ELECTRIFIED

50 YEARS OF ELECTRIC FACTORY

TABLE OF CONTENTS

Catalog for *Electrified: 50 Years of Electric Factory* exhibition
September 22 – December 30, 2023
Paul Peck Alumni Center and Bossone Research Center
Drexel University
Published by Drexel University 2023

Contributors:
Joe Amon
Kaisha Blackstone
Derek Gillman
R. Scott Hanson
Sam Katz
Youngmoo Kim
Lynn Waddell
Eric Zillmer

Design: Fiona Tran, Mark Willie

ISBN: 978-1-936484-07-2

PREFACE

In his anthemic song "Thunder Road," Bruce Springsteen
captured the adventurous, electrifying spirit of rock and roll
music when he proclaimed, "I got this guitar and I learned how
to make it talk."

And now, Drexel University is hosting "Electrified: 50
Years of the Electric Factory," a compelling exhibition
that practically sings to us about an era that enriched
Philadelphia's collective musical heritage and cemented our
city's place in rock history. Through posters, photographs and
artifacts, we learn how Philadelphia played an integral part
in the careers of legendary musical artists like Springsteen,
Jimi Hendrix, Janis Joplin, Tina Turner, David Bowie, Bob
Dylan, and Amy Winehouse. We recall the memorable live
performances that they and other legendary bands and solo
acts delivered in iconic Philadelphia venues, from the intimate
Electric Factory to the Spectrum and on to the site of the 1985
Live Aid Concert, JFK Stadium. We revisit a turbulent period
in history when singer-songwriters gave voice to protest and to
changes in popular culture. And we meet Larry Magid, a Philly
boy-turned-visionary musical entrepreneur and impresario
who transformed a tire factory into the Electric Factory, the
city's first beloved rock venue, before revolutionizing live
music promotion globally through Electric Factory Concerts.

No exhibit can possibly capture the sounds and excitement
from a half century's worth of live performances. Nor can it
do justice to the singular entrepreneurial genius behind this
glorious chapter in Philadelphia's collective musical history.
But as long as more people come to appreciate what the
Electric Factory meant to this city, to popular music, and to
the artists who made the music, I am sure Larry Magid will be
most grateful.

I am certainly grateful to Margery Sly, Joe Lucia, President
JoAnne Epps, and all our friends at Larry's alma mater,
Temple University, for graciously providing most of the
graphic materials from Temple's Special Collections Research
Center that are on display.

John Fry, President
Drexel University

01

POLITICS IN THE 1960s

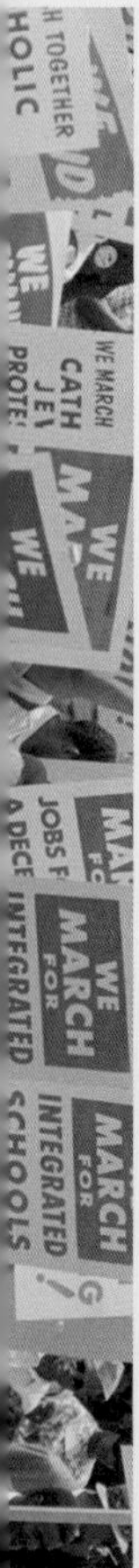

Fig. 1

Fig. 2

9 NOVEMBER 1962

RT AREA

Fig. 2

UNCOVERED LAUNCHER

CANVAS COVERED LAUNCHER

Fig. 3

THE 1960s BEGAN WITH A SENSE OF OPTIMISM

and idealism among a new generation of young people inspired by President John F. Kennedy and the Civil Rights movement, but the specter of nuclear war and Vietnam loomed — especially after the Cuban Missile Crisis, and the Gulf of Tonkin incident when President Lyndon B. Johnson declared war on North Vietnam.

The Student Non-Violent Coordinating Committee of Black students drew on the principles of Rev. Dr. Martin Luther King, Jr. (and Gandhi before him), which in turn influenced the "Port Huron Statement," a manifesto written in 1962 by Students for a Democratic Society (SDS). Student unrest gathered momentum as chapters of SDS popped up all over the country. The student movement effectively began at the University of California-Berkeley, followed by the first "teach-in" about the war in Vietnam at the University of Michigan.

We are people of this generation,

"PORT HURON STATEMENT" 1962

Fig. 4

bred in at least modest comfort, housed now in universities, looking uncomfortably to the world we inherit.

When we were kids the United States was the wealthiest and strongest country in the world; the only one with the atom bomb, the least scarred by modern war, an initiator of the United Nations that we thought would distribute Western influence throughout the world. Freedom and equality for each individual, government of, by, and for the people – these American values we found good, principles by which we could live as men. Many of us began maturing in complacency.

As we grew, however, our comfort was penetrated by events too troubling to dismiss. First, the permeating and victimizing fact of human degradation, symbolized by the Southern struggle against racial bigotry, compelled most of us from silence to activism. Second, the enclosing fact of the Cold War, symbolized by the presence of the Bomb, brought awareness that we ourselves, and our friends, and millions of abstract "others" we knew more directly because of our common peril, might die at any time. We might deliberately ignore, or avoid, or fail to feel all other human problems, but not these two, for these were too immediate and crushing in their impact, too challenging in the demand that we as individuals take the responsibility for encounter and resolution.

Fig. 5

Fig. 6

Fig. 7

Fig. 8

President Johnson pursued a policy of gradual escalation in Vietnam, but official news accounts from the Pentagon did not mesh with circulated facts: the body count was solemnly read every night by Walter Cronkite on CBS News. The anti-war movement grew more militant, seeking to "bring the war home." At the same time, there were race riots in major cities, including Philadelphia, New York and Los Angeles. In 1966, the year after the assassination of Malcolm X, Stokely Carmichael called for "Black Power" and the Black Panther Party for Self Defense formed in Oakland, California.

Musicians took note of these changing times, and sought to reflect them or escape them, in folk and rock songs.

02

CULTURAL REVOLUTION

ASIDE FROM PROTESTS FOR CIVIL RIGHTS and against Vietnam, targets of the widespread rebellion among younger Americans included consumerism and the conformity of the nuclear family. This revolution had begun on a smaller scale in the 1950s with the Beat writers, among them poet Allen Ginsberg and novelist Jack Kerouac. Communes founded by hippies committed to an anti-capitalist, organic lifestyle and the adoption of handmade objects. Members of the older generation mostly regarded this as escapism, as they did the widespread use of hallucinogenic drugs, notably d-lysergic acid (LSD).

One significant component of this rejection of post-WWII materialism was an attraction to traditions and beliefs beyond Europe. Jimi Hendrix and Rita Coolidge celebrated their Cherokee heritage by sometimes wearing beaded clothes to perform on stage.

The Beatles helped focus attention on Asia. George Harrison first visited India in 1966, the year he began studying with Indian sitar player Ravi Shankar. Two years later the band practiced Transcendental Meditation under the Hindu guru (teacher) Maharishi Mahesh Yogi at his ashram by the Ganges River—an event widely covered by the western media.

This "turn to the East" was accompanied by a turn inwards, of which drugs were a part. Iran, Afghanistan, India and Nepal became destinations on the "hippie trail". An early champion of LSD, Harvard psychologist Richard Alpert first traveled to India in 1967, subsequently advancing the practice of mindfulness in the West as the guru Ram Dass. Hinduism, Buddhism and Sufism all found young American and British adherents.

Fig. 1

lalat - 1429. b. 674 - 267182 ?

Fig. 2

11

"turn to

the East"

03

THE ELECTRIC *GUITAR*

AMERICA GAVE BIRTH TO THE ELECTRIC GUITAR,

of which the best-known manufacturers are Gibson and Fender.

In the mid-1930s, the well-established Gibson Co. added magnetic coils ("pickups") beneath the strings of its jazz guitars, converting vibrations into electric signals, which then fed into an amplifier to make the instrument louder. Leo Fender, who started out in Fullerton, California, repairing and making radios, PA systems and amplifiers, began to build his own electric guitars during the 1940s.

Fender, Gibson, and other leading electric guitar manufacturers like Gretsch, Guild and Rickenbacker, sought to outdo one another, especially after 1951, the year in which Fender introduced the world's first solid-body guitar: the Telecaster (Bruce Springsteen's Telecaster is displayed in the exhibition). Prior to this, electric guitars had followed the general form of hollow-bodied stringed instruments, often with f-holes like violins and cellos.

Fender's instruments changed the guitar world and helped define the sound and look of rock. Its Stratocaster (the "Strat"), famously played by Jimi Hendrix, had a comfortable double-cutaway contour, and an expressive tone created by three single-coil pickups plus a tremolo/vibrato arm that instantly changed the string pitch.

As protest movements became more strident in the mid-late 1960s, popular music changed with the times. The cleaner, innocent rock of the 1950s grew darker and psychedelic with guitarists adding distortion and other effects in the '60s. Folk music changed forever when Bob Dylan plugged in a sunburst Strat at the Newport Folk Festival in 1965.

Fig. 1

Fig. 2

17

04

Fig. 1

ELECTRIC FACTORY

Fig. 2

LATE 1967 WOULD PROVE TO BE A

transformative moment in the musical history of Philadelphia, which was the site of American Bandstand, Doo Wop groups, and a thriving jazz scene. The stage was set for a new kind of performance venue for the increasingly important genre of rock music. By this time, bands were getting louder and outgrowing smaller venues.

After working as a talent agent in New York, representing the brightest upcoming musicians of the mid-1960s, Larry Magid returned to Philadelphia and connected with brothers Allen, Herb and Jerry Spivak, and Shelly Kaplan. Herb Spivak already owned a jazz nightspot called the Showboat Theatr (sic) but was keen to harness Larry Magid's experience in promoting rock musicians. The two began discussing plans to open a club that would be a hip underground environment for rock.

Fig. 3

Fig. 4

"Clapton @ Electric Factory 1968" © J. Pardu

Electric Factory's first home would be a vacant warehouse at 22nd and Arch streets, and the team quickly went to work transforming it with the help of art students, who not only painted the walls psychedelically but also the Factory's Cadillac parked outside.

Opening on Feb. 2, 1968, with the Chambers Brothers singing appropriately: "Time has come today," and playwright Tennessee Williams in the audience, the 2,500 seat Electric Factory helped put Philadelphia on the map as another epicenter of the counterculture, and a fixture in the concert industry. It offered DayGlo face-painting, strobe lights, incense, patchouli water, mirrored canvas tunnels, and benches created as coffins. As Larry Magid said: "the name has lasted, and the logo — Ben Franklin with long hair and granny glasses — was perfect. "It just fit.""

Fig. 6

Fig. 5

05

Fig. 1

ELECTRIC FACTORY CONCERTS

Fig. 2

GROWING OUT OF THE PARTNERSHIP THAT

created Electric Factory on Arch Street
in 1968, Electric Factory Concerts (EFC)
became the largest popular music promoter
in the USA.

Having mounted the Quaker City Jazz
Festival at the Spectrum arena in 1967,
Herb Spivak gave Larry Magid the idea
that many rock acts would also benefit
from larger spaces. The Spectrum was
a new sports venue with the capacity to
host music concerts on nights the Flyers
or Sixers weren't playing, which provided
additional, needed income. It could also be
divided, creating a more intimate space for
performers who weren't prepared to play in
front of 20,000 people.

EFC also presented free summer shows
("be-ins") on Belmont Plateau in Fairmount
Park, which attracted thousands of
attendees when the non-air-conditioned
Electric Factory was closed. These "be-
ins" and the Spectrum concerts paved the
way for yet larger shows at JFK Stadium
including Live Aid in 1985, which EFC co-
produced (featured in this exhibition).

Two years after the original Electric
Factory closed, EFC opened another club-
like space, the Bijou Cafe at 1409 Lombard
St.: a place to go all week (even on Sundays,
in the face of "blue laws" prohibiting the sale
of alcohol). Acts would have a residency up
to five days, and it was a catalyst for up-and-
coming talent both in music and comedy.
EFC also acquired Theatre of Living Arts
(TLA), which helped revitalize South Street,
and the more capacious Tower Theater in
Upper Darby.

Fig. 3

DAN HICKS & HIS HOT LICKS

Bijou Caters To 'Hip' Crowd

PHILADELPHIA — The cafe had its opening on Wednesday, Oct. 4. The Bijou is located in a building at 1409 Lombard St., which once housed the Showboat Theatre, a mecca for jazz enthusiasts during the 1950s and early 1960s, and most recently the discotheque Chances are.

The Bijou will be the city's only night spot presenting top-name artists who appeal to a "hip" 21 years and over audience.

Premier entertainers in the fields of progressive rock, jazz, folk, blues and the "new-comedy" will be showcased Wednesdays through Saturdays.

The Bijou will accomodate 250 persons on two levels. The lower level with seat 150 at long tables. Food

and spirits will be served including imported wines and beers, jumbo pitchers of sangria, Bloody Mary's, and Apple Annie's (a house specialty made from apple juice and rum).

Performances will be at 8:30 and 11 p.m. weekdays; 9 and 11:30 p.m. Friday, and 8:30, 10:30 and 12:30 p.m. Saturday.

Opening the Bijou will be Dan Hicks and His Hot Licks and Whole Oats. Wed. Oct. 4 through Sat., Oct. 7. David Clayton Thomas, formerly lead singer with Blood Sweat & Tears, appears Oct. 11-14, followed by Mort Sahl, Oct. 18-21. Future bookings include Weather Report and Good God. Nov. 1-5, and Seatrain at a yet-to-be-determined date.

The Bijou is operated by

Larry Magid and Allen Spivak of Electric Factory Concerts.

Fig. 4

06

Fig. 1

1969 ATLANTIC CITY POP FESTIVAL AND WOODSTOCK

Fig. 2

Atlantic City Pop Festival
AUGUST 1·2·3
Atlantic City Race Track/Atlantic City, N.J.

Friday · Aug. 1 · Iron Butterfly · Procol Harum
Crosby, Stills & Nash · Booker T & the M. G.'s
Joni Mitchell · Chicago · Santana Blues Band
Johnny Winter ·

Saturday · Aug. 2 · Jefferson Airplane · Glen McKay's Headlights
Creedence Clearwater · Lighthouse ·
Crazy World of Arthur Brown · B. B. King ·
Butterfield Blues Band · Tim Buckley
Byrds · Hugh Masekela · American Dream

Sunday · Aug. 3 · Janis Joplin · Canned Heat
Mothers of Invention · Sir Douglass Quintet
3 Dog Night · "Dr. John" the Night Tripper ·
Joe Cocker · Buddy Rich Big Band
· Little Richard ·
· Moody Blues ·

Music · Carnival and
3-Day Exposition

Advance tickets:
$6. per performance
$15. for all 3 performances.
Tickets at door:
$6.75 per performance.
For additional information call:
The Electric Factory
LO 3-9284
Atlantic City Race Track
(609) 646-5002

MANY AMERICANS HAVE HEARD OF THE

Woodstock Festival in 1969, held in upstate New York. However, Electric Factory Concerts (EFC) followed its "be-ins" in Fairmount Park by organizing one of the largest and most successful of 1969's outdoor festicals: the Atlantic City Pop Festival, which ran from Aug. 1–3, two weeks before Woodstock.

Outdoor music festivals began in the mid-to-late 1950s, with the Newport Jazz and Folk Festivals, and California's Monterey Jazz Festival. The first devoted to rock was the Monterey International Pop Festival mounted in 1967, during the "Summer of Love."

By 1969, racetracks were the preferred venue for rock festivals because they offered ticketed entry and more security, and Herb Spivak made a deal to hold EFC's three-day festical at the Atlantic City Race Course. A stage designed by architect Buckminster Fuller revolved on a turntable in order to reduce the wait time between performances. Tickets were $6 per day or $15 for all three.

Because the bands' managers specified that no audio or video recordings were allowed, the Atlantic City Pop Festival lives on mainly in the memory of those who attended. It was much better organized than Woodstock, without the mud and traffic, and had an equally impressive lineup that concluded with fiery performances by Janis Joplin and Little Richard.

The following year, EFC planned a similarly ambitious festival (Harmonyville) at Walpack in rural New Jersey, but with the acts already booked it was canceled after protests from local residents.

Fig. 3

07

RHYTHM, *BEAT* AND THE *INFLUENCE* OF *AFRICA*

Fig. 1

THE SOUNDS OF AFRICAN MUSIC AND ITS

culture have clear influences in American music and its history. Complex rhythms and melodies, which stretch the bounds of the western tonal scale, are woven into the American genres of jazz, blues, soul and rock.

The "backbeat" that Chuck Berry sang about is what gives rock its driving, irresistible force. With strong accents on the second and fourth beat of every bar, backbeat featured in rhythm and blues, Delta blues, New Orleans jazz, foot-tapping and hand-clapping in spirituals and shouts, and work songs of the enslaved. It ultimately derived from percussive rhythms in West Africa.

Black musicians like Chuck Berry, Little Richard, Bo Diddley and Fats Domino played 'rock and roll' which crossed over with white audiences in segregated America. To other African Americans it was known as rhythm and blues, or R&B. The genre developed after blues guitarist Muddy Waters moved from the Mississippi Delta to Chicago in 1944 and switched to electric guitar backed by a band with drums, bass, rhythm guitar, and harmonica.

By the late 1960s, rock bands, as well as the venues where they performed, were becoming more racially integrated. The backbeat found its way into other genres — from heavy metal to reggae, punk, rap, and grunge.

Fig. 2

ELVIS PRESLEY AND PHILADELPHIAN

Bill Haley were among the white musicians who listened to "race music" on the radio. They found success by adapting rock and roll for white teenagers — sometimes by fusing it with country music — which scared many parents, who associated the new sound with juvenile delinquency and also interracial audiences.

Continuing to blend African, Spanish and American cultural influences, with Jamaican street talk and rock guitar, Bob Marley and the Wailers played the Bijou Café in 1973 and 1975, and opened their Rastaman Vibration Tour at the Tower Theater in April 1976, playing two shows. They later returned to the Spectrum in June 1978, where, by then, reggae and other African-influenced forms attracted a diverse audience in the Philadelphia music scene.

Afrobeat, whose creation is attributed to the Nigerian composer and musician Fela Kuti in the 1960s, is a fusion of traditional Yoruba music, jazz, funk, soul and Highlife. Decades later, Grammy winner and Philadelphia native Bilal recorded a remake of Kuti's 1977 "Sorrow, Tears and Blood" from his unreleased "Love for Sale" album.

The Afrobeat sound can be characterized by its polyrhythmic percussion, improvisation and seamless integration of several musical styles. Artists such as jazz trumpeter Hugh Masekela, whose hit "Grazing in the Grass" imports South African percussive elements with jazz instrumentation, solidified this musical fusion in Philadelphia culture. The Spivak brothers had headlined him at concerts even before the opening of Electric Factory, where he played in April 1968.

THE BAMBOULA.

Fig. 3

33

08

Fig. 1

LIVE AID

Fig. 2

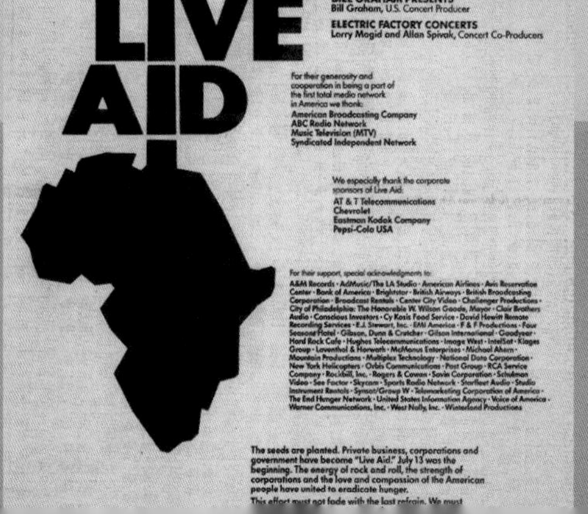

THE LIVE AID FOUNDATION
extends our deepest appreciation to those who created
LIVE AID — the world's most star-studded rock concert, the
largest television event in history, and, most significantly,
the African famine relief benefit to unite the family of man.

Our special thanks to:

BOB GELDOF
The founder of Band Aid and
the spirit and force behind Live Aid

HARVEY GOLDSMITH
Live Aid Concert Producer

WORLDWIDE SPORTS AND ENTERTAINMENT
Michael C. Mitchell, President and Executive Producer
Hal Uplinger, Vice-President and Producer
Tony Verna, Executive Director

BILL GRAHAM PRESENTS
Bill Graham, U.S. Concert Producer

ELECTRIC FACTORY CONCERTS
Larry Magid and Allan Spivak, Concert Co-Producers

for their generosity and
cooperation in being a part of
the first total media network
in America we thank:
American Broadcasting Company
ABC Radio Network
Music Television (MTV)
Syndicated Independent Network

We especially thank the corporate
sponsors of Live Aid:

AT & T Telecommunications
Chevrolet
Eastman Kodak Company
Pepsi-Cola USA

For their support, special acknowledgments to:
A&M Records · AdMusic/The LA Studio · American Airlines · Avis Reservation
Center · Bank of America · Brightstar · British Airways · British Broadcasting
Corporation · Broadcast Rentals · Center City Video · Challenger Productions ·
City of Philadelphia: The Honorable W. Wilson Goode, Mayor · Clair Brothers
Audio · Canadian Investors · Cy Rasis Food Service · David Hewitt Remote
Recording Services · F.J. Stewart, Inc. · EMI America · F & F Productions · Four
Seasons Hotel · Gibson, Dunn & Crutcher · Gilson International · Goodyear ·
Hard Rock Cafe · Hughes Telecommunications · Image West · IntelSat · Kings
Group · Lowenthal & Horwath · MaHanns Enterprises · Michael Ahern ·
Mountain Productions · Multiplex Technology · National Data Corporation ·
New Twist Helicopters · Orbis Communications · Port Group · RCA Service
Company · Recolodi, Inc. · Rogers & Cowan · Sonix Corporation · Schieiman
Video · See Factor · Skycam · Sports Radio Network · Starfleet Audio · Studio
Instrument Rentals · Synsvt/Group W · Telemarketing Corporation of America ·
The End Hunger Network · United States Information Agency · Voice of America ·
Werner Communications, Inc. · West Nally, Inc. · Winterland Productions

The seeds are planted. Private business, corporations and
government have become "Live Aid." July 13 was the
beginning. The energy of rock and roll, the strength of
corporations and the love and compassion of the American
people have united to eradicate hunger.
This effort must not fade with the last refrain. We must

THE WALL STREET JOURNAL, FRIDAY, JULY 19, 198...

IN THE FIRST HALF OF THE 1980S, ETHIOPIA

was subject to one of the world's worst-ever famines, estimated to have taken the lives of up to a million people.

Shortly after coordinating the 1984 release of the single "Do They Know It's Christmas?" to raise funds for Ethiopia, Bob Geldof of the Irish band the Boomtown Rats formulated a truly ambitious plan. He drove forward an idea for two major charity concerts — to be held simultaneously in England and America — that could help alleviate starvation in Ethiopia and its east African neighbor Sudan. Geldof worked with producer Harvey Goldsmith on London's Wembley Stadium concert, and with Larry Magid and Allen Spivak of Electric Factory Concerts who, together with San Francisco-based promoter Bill Graham, produced the show at Philadelphia's JFK Stadium.

Such was the passion and urgent need for this remarkable project that the period from the decision to stage the U.S. show in Philadelphia to its realization was less than six weeks. The American show had to be on the East Coast, in order that the two broadcasts could be linked in any viable way, yet Live Aid still posed a massive technical challenge, with satellites transmitting live performances at a time before digital equipment was in use.

The concerts were broadcast from London and Philadelphia on July 13, 1985, to over a 100 countries around the world. Beginning at Wembley and continuing at JFK, where 90,000 people attended, Live Aid was watched by more than a billion people. It is estimated that Live Aid eventually contributed over $100 million dollars for famine relief in east Africa.

Fig. 3

09

CLAIR BROS. AUDIO

Fig. 1

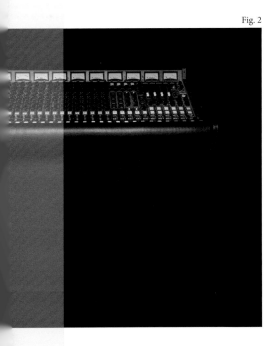

Fig. 2

THE NEED FOR ADEQUATE CONCERT SOUND

was underlined in 1965 by the Beatles' performance at Shea Stadium, New York, when the band couldn't be heard above their screaming fans. In the 1960s and '70s, new technologies for high-power sound amplification and reinforcement enabled the success of stadium concerts.

One of the pioneering companies spearheading this development was founded by two brothers, Roy and Gene Clair from Lititz, Pennsylvania. After their public address (PA) system was used by Frankie Valli and the Four Seasons for a show at Franklin & Marshall College in 1966, the brothers were invited to provide speakers for subsequent performances. In 1968, their speakers were used at Cream's Spectrum show, produced by Electric Factory Concerts, who continued to use Clair systems for other bands.

The Clair S4 all-in-one PA speaker was introduced in 1974 and became a mainstay in large venues for decades. The single box design (45 by 45 inches) includes ten speakers overall: two 18-inch bass speakers, four 10-inch midrange drivers, two 2-inch high frequency speakers with horns, and two ultra-high frequency drivers. Each unit offers hundreds of watts of power and outputs an enormous amount of acoustic energy. Although each box weighs 425 pounds, they can be stacked or suspended on a grid to form the visual "wall of sound" often seen at large performance spaces.

First used on tour by Rod Stewart, the S4 system was adopted by the Rolling Stones, the Beach Boys and many other bands throughout the 1970s. Clair also provided sound reinforcement for Live Aid at JFK Stadium.

10

WHY MUSIC?

Fig. 1

why do we dance to music?
why does music evoke such
strong emotions and memories?
why is there rhythm in music?
and why is there music?

Fig. 2

PHILOSOPHER THEODORE ADORNO SUGGESTED

that "we don't understand music...music understands us."

Our entire species plays and listens to music, with scholarship suggesting that music is important in experiencing human life and creativity. In fact, half of all Nobel Prize winners report that they play a musical instrument.

The brain is an amazingly complicated, but ultimately beautiful, three-pound organ which has evolved to play a central role in the human body — not only in sustaining the life of its owner, but also in playing a Fender Stratocaster. Everything musical is simultaneously biological, but how does the brain process sound to experience music?

Surprisingly, there is no specific music center in the brain and, remarkably, music is processed, imagined, and understood everywhere in the brain. It is a neuropsychological fact that when you play the guitar you use many different regions in your brain. It's busier than a traffic intersection at Rittenhouse Square. Neuropsychologically, in the words of Metallica, "Nothing Else Matters."

Because emotions enhance memory processes and music evokes strong emotions, music is neurologically involved in forming memories. That is why we remember a melody, for example, even after many years. So, when we give the gift of music, we present an offering of memories and emotions, not only of the music itself but of events associated with hearing and playing it.

41

11

GUITARS AND RHYTHM

"THE ONLY TIME I'M HAPPY'S WHEN I play

my guitar," from "N.S.U.," written by Jack Bruce and recorded on the Fender Bass VI displayed in the exhibition for Cream's first album, "Fresh Cream."

EEG brain wave studies found that guitar players synchronize neurologically as well as rhythmically when they jam together. Cream was known for its extended jam sets. Jack Bruce and Ginger Baker clashed both onstage and offstage, but in performance, together with Eric Clapton, their brains appear to have worked together well.

Like other instruments, the guitar has specific cognitive and emotional features: it requires a high degree of sequencing, multi-tasking, planning, synchronization, motor speed and neuro-emotional modulation. Therefore, learning the guitar can be difficult. It helps that the brain has mirror neurons, a certain type of brain cell involved in learning a skill by watching others, which is the easiest way to pick up playing the guitar — whether from a friend, a teacher or YouTube. Priced at as little as $100, the guitar is among the most popular instruments in the world. It is portable, and left-handers are invited: five percent of all Martin guitars are produced for left-handers; zero percent of Steinway pianos are made for left-handers.

Attending a concert and listening to music allows us to temporarily set aside anxieties and focus on the moment, which for psychologists is a key ingredient of happiness.

Fig. 1

Fig. 2

Fig. 3

12

RHYTHM, POETRY AND LYRICS

Fig. 1

IT CAN BE ARGUED THAT RHYTHM IN ITSELF,

rather than melody, defines the DNA of popular music since there is no melody without rhythm. Mozart suggested that "music is not in the notes, but in the silence between." Two notes create a space-time continuum between them, which can be seen as the basis of rhythm: a systematic pattern of musical sounds.

Different music genres have different speeds, or beats-per-minute (bpm). Electronic dance music (EDM) is typically 128 bpm, but spa music is close to zero bpm. Adjusting the tempo is one of the easiest ways to change the mood of the music and therefore the neurochemistry of your brain.

Speech — and especially poetry — conveys emotional intentions through rhythm. This can be easily seen in the genre of rap music, formed almost exclusively of words with a strong rhythmic beat, typically recorded between speeds of 80 and 100 bpm (a sweet spot for rap). Sometimes, poetry and music come together in a beautiful weaving of rhythmic sounds and words, as they do with singer-songwriter Bob Dylan, who has not only won 10 Grammy awards for his music, but also the 2016 Nobel Prize for literature.

Rhythm, timing, and the anticipation of timing, is all-important to music. Rhythm is one key to creativity: our own personal journey, and the anticipation of what comes next. Our lives are, perhaps, like an extended drum solo.

Fig. 2

Fig. 3

It ain't no use to sit and wonder why, babe
It don't matter, anyhow
An' it ain't no use to sit and wonder why, babe
If you don't know by now
When your rooster crows at the break of dawn
Look out your window and I'll be gone
You're the reason I'm trav'lin' on
Don't think twice, it's all right

— Bob Dylan, first verse of "Don't think twice,
it's alright", 1962, released 1963

13

Fig. 1

2nd
ELECTRIC FACTORY
AND LIVE 8

Fig. 2

TWENTY-FIVE YEARS AFTER THE ORIGINAL

Electric Factory closed, it was reborn in 1995 at 421 N. 7th St. in a converted warehouse that was, as if by Divine Providence, once part of the General Electric Switchgear Plant. Incorporating some of the psychedelic atmosphere of the original venue, the new Electric Factory still provided an 'experience' but one that catered to different generations of concert goers. The second Factory was managed by Allen Spivak's son, Adam.

The lineups were eclectic, with performances by established stars, like Prince, Patti Smith and Bob Dylan, as well as younger performers emerging from the region, including the neo-soul artists Bilal, Musiq Soulchild, Jill Scott and Vivian Green. The 3,000-capacity space was both intimate but big enough to create the feeling of excitement found at stadium shows, yet with no seat restrictions. Fans could get as close to the stage as they were willing to push.

Two decades after the success of Live Aid, U2's lead singer Bono joined Bob Geldof to focus leaders at the 2005 G8 Summit on world poverty and debt forgiveness. To create Live 8, they collaborated again with the producers of Live Aid: London promoter Harvey Goldsmith and Electric Factory Concerts. This time it was to be an international series of 10 concerts mounted on July 2, days before the G8 Summit began. The major stages were again in London and Philadelphia, plus eight other cities around the world. A final concert took place on July 6 in Edinburgh, Scotland, the day before the G8 leaders gathered.

Fig. 3

Fig. 4

Fig. 5

Fig. 6

14

LIVE AID
LIVE 8
AND *FAMINE RELIEF*

Fig. 1

IN 1981, FOUR YEARS BEFORE LIVE AID,

the economist Amartya Sen published a book titled "Poverty and Famines: An Essay on Entitlement and Deprivation." The book analyzed the causes of famines in India, Bangladesh and the Sahel region of Africa. Sen found that famine was less the result of food shortages and more a consequence of (lack of) rights and power.

Attempts to address famine that focus only on food supply may succeed in saving some lives but come too late to save many and do little to prevent future catastrophes. Nonetheless, Live Aid and Live 8 shone a light on government abuses and inspired many people to try and understand the more complicated causes of famine, which include autocratic regimes, oppressive policies and the foreigners who support them.

Major causes of food insecurity in the Sahel region today include conflict and climate change. Globally, 43 million people are at risk of famine. Compared to 1985, the world is better able to monitor food insecurity, but the solutions are still complex. In emergency settings, food assistance can save lives. Strengthening education, nutrition, livelihood resilience and social protection systems help in the longer term, as do protecting rights.

Drexel's Dana and David Dornsife School of Public Health, founded on the belief that health is a human right, is partnering with researchers and development workers across Africa, increasing understanding of effective health interventions and building local capacity for sustainable development.

15

LARRY MAGID AND *ELECTRIC FACTORY*

Fig. 1

Fig. 2

Fig. 3

TAKEN BY HIS FATHER TO A MOVIE AT THE

Earle Theatre on Market Street, eight-year-old Larry Magid was mesmerized by what followed: a big band performing on the theater stage, carried up by hydraulic lift.

It could be said that his career as a promoter began in 1958 at the WDAS radio station where, after fetching cheesesteaks for DJ Julian Graham, he was offered the opportunity to introduce a record. As a young entrepreneur, Magid first booked performers to play at college fraternity parties: $150 for the band and $15 for the promoter. With a voice in the tradition of Nat King Cole, Lee Andrews (father of Roots drummer and Philly native Questlove) was one of his early acts, singing "Long Lonely Nights," "Teardrops" and "Try the Impossible." Their three-year partnership captured the sound of Philadelphia before it became a brand.

The creation of Electric Factory was underpinned by Larry Magid's experience in New York in the mid-Sixties at the General Artists talent agency, when he was responsible for securing performers still relatively unknown in the U.S., like Jimi Hendrix and Cream, who became the bedrock at Arch Street.

His personal passion for, and deep knowledge of popular music led him over the decades to encourage hundreds of performers. At the same time, he and his partners Allen, Herb and Jerry Spivak, along with Shelley Kaplan, were acutely aware that concerts were not only an experience for the audience — music allied to ever more sophisticated sound systems and light shows — but also a business.

ELECTRIFIED

50 YEARS OF ELECTRIC FACTORY

FENDER ESQUIRE-TELECASTER, 1953–54

Ash body, maple neck, two single-coil pickups

When introduced in 1950, Fender's first solid body guitar had a single-coil pickup at the guitar's bridge. Named the "Esquire," it was followed very shortly by a model with two pickups, which was initially called the "Broadcaster" and then the "Telecaster." Although Esquires could be readily turned into Telecasters by installing a second pickup at the neck, this iconic instrument instead combines an Esquire neck and Telecaster body.

It was Bruce Springsteen's principal guitar for thirty years, from 1972 on. When he bought it from a New Jersey guitar store in 1972, the body had been further hollowed out — to allow a unique configuration of four pickups — making it lighter than conventional Telecasters and more comfortable to play during long concerts. The separate components and modifications led to its nickname, "Mutt."

Seen on the "Born to Run" album cover, it has been played in Philadelphia more than any other high-profile electric instrument.

| On loan from Bruce Springsteen

BRUCE SPRINGSTEEN, AUG. 14–15, 1985

JFK Stadium, Philadelphia, PA
Photo by Zohrab Kazanjian, 1985

| On loan from Special Collections and Research Center, Temple University

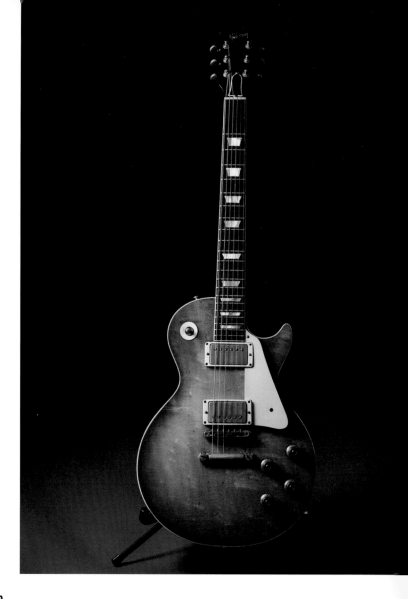

GIBSON LES PAUL STANDARD, 1958

Mahogany body and neck, maple top, rosewood
fingerboard, two humbucking pickups

Gibson was established at the beginning of the
20th century in Kalamazoo, Michigan. Among the
most coveted vintage electric guitars today are
its solid-bodied Les Paul models built between
the years 1957 and 1962, which featured the first
"Patent Applied For" (P.A.F.) noise-cancelling or
hum-bucking pickups, known as humbuckers.

This 1958 Les Paul Standard was owned by Mick
Taylor, who played it at the Spectrum in 1972
during the Rolling Stones' U.S. tour (the original
P.A.F. humbuckers have since been replaced).
Although Mick Taylor and Keith Richards shared
more than one Les Paul in the early 1970s, this is
most likely the guitar held by drummer Charlie
Watts on the cover of the band's 1970 live album
"Get Yer Ya-Ya's Out."

| On loan from Hard Rock International

FENDER BASS VI, 1962

Alder body, maple neck, rosewood fingerboard,
three single-coil pickups

Painted by Marijke Koger and Simon Posthuma of
"The Fool Collective", London, 1967

Jack Bruce used this six-string bass to record
Cream's first album, "Fresh Cream" (1966). It
was then painted in 1967 in preparation Cream's
European and American tours.

Fool Collective was formed in London in 1967 by
Dutch psychedelic artist-designers Marijke Koger,
Simon Posthuma and Josje Leeger, together with
Leeger's partner Barry Finch. As well as painting
the Fender Bass VI and Eric Clapton's 1964
Gibson SG guitar (which came to be known as
"The Fool"), Fool also designed stage clothes for
the band.

When Cream played at the Electric Factory in
April 1968, Eric Clapton played both his painted
Gibson SG and the Gibson Firebird he'd just
purchased from a Philadelphia music store. Jack
Bruce, however, used a four-string Gibson EB-3 on
stage, reserving the painted bass principally for
TV shows.

| On loan from Hard Rock International

61

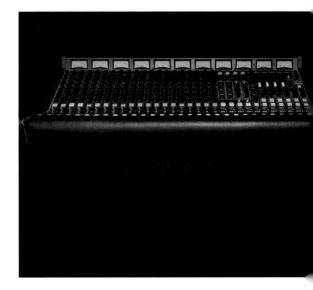

CLAIR BROS. CUSTOM CONSOLE / "THE ELVIS BOARD," CA. 1971

Designed by Bruce Jackson of Clair Bros., this custom-made console used circuitry from SAE. According to Clair engineers, it was a nightmare to ground correctly, and the power supplies blew up regularly. The console was used by Jackson on tour with Elvis Presley earning it the nickname, "The Elvis Board." After the CBA-32, or "Clair Console," was unveiled in 1977, this board was moved from front-of-house to the monitor mix position.

| On loan from Clair Global

FENDER DELUXE REVERB AMPLIFIER, 1967
Fullerton, CA

First introduced in 1963, the Deluxe Reverb has been used extensively both in studio and live settings. Because of its innovative features and relatively light weight for a stage amplifier, it has often been called the "desert island amp," which many guitarists would pick if they had only one choice. The Deluxe Reverb has one 12" speaker, capacity to generate reverberation effects through a spring-driven "reverb tank," two channels (one featuring vibrato), and 22 watts of power driven by two 6V6 vacuum tubes.

This particular amp was made by Fender Musical Instruments in April 1967, the last year of the so-called "blackface" Fender amps featuring a black control panel with white lettering before Fender switched to "silverface" with blue lettering in 1968 — one of several changes to the product line after Leo Fender sold his company to Columbia Broadcasting System (CBS) in 1965.

| On loan from R. Scott Hanson

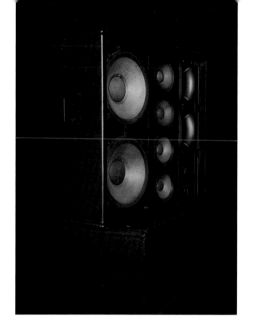

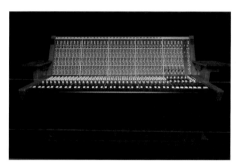

CLAIR BROS. S4 ALL-IN-ONE PA (PUBLIC ADDRESS) SPEAKER, 1974

The Clair S4 all-in-one PA (public address) speaker became a mainstay in large venues for decades. Each unit offers hundreds of watts of power and outputs an enormous amount of acoustic energy.

| On loan from Clair Global

CLAIR BROS. CBA-32 MIXING CONSOLE / "THE CLAIR CONSOLE," 1977

Clair Bros. engineers Bruce Jackson and Ron Borthwick began work on the Clair Console in 1974. This revolutionary board made its official debut in 1977. The CBA-32 Mixing Console was the first live mixing console to come equipped with parametric equalization. Among its other distinct features were a folding design and plasma RMS/peak level meters. Nine more Clair Consoles were manufactured between 1977 and 1982 and it remained a revered live mixing board well into the 1990's. Today, it stands as a testament to Clair's commitment to boldly advancing technology-driven experiences.

| On loan from Clair Global

SAE MARK II AMPLIFIER, CA 1967

The SAE Mark II Amplifier was one of the first widely adopted solid-state amplifiers. Clair Bros. had a strong relationship with SAE founder Morris Kessler and used the Mark II Amplifier and a handful of other SAE products and components during the 1970's.

| On loan from Clair Global

CLAIR BROS. COHERENT TRANSFER SYSTEM OR "CTS," 1990

The Clair Coherent Transfer System (or "CTS") is an analog crossover/limiter system that was designed specifically for the S4 Series II 4-way loudspeaker. Engineers Greg Oshiro, Ron Borthwick and Rick Lehman lent their expertise to the project. The CTS made its debut on tour with Robert Plant in 1990.

| On loan from Clair Global

JIMI HENDRIX "CASE CANDY" ACCOMPANYING 1969 FENDER STRATOCASTER
Santa Ana, CA, 1969

"Case candy" is a nickname given by guitarists to the documentation and information that comes with a new instrument, placed within the case.

| On loan from R. Scott Hanson

Not Pictured

MARSHALL STACK, COMPRISING 1974 50-WATT AMPLIFIER HEAD WITH 1976 CABINETS: "1960A" (TOP) AND "1960B" (BOTTOM)
England

British-manufactured Marshall stacks are among the most iconic amplification systems in rock and roll. With truly powerful sound projection, the first was designed by Jim Marshall in 1965 at the request of the Who's Pete Townshend, who wanted a system that could fill bigger venues. At Townshend's insistence, Marshall packed eight 12" (diameter) speakers within one cabinet. This was so heavy as to be unusable by the band's road crew. The engineer then returned to his original conception of fitting four 12" speakers into a cabinet.

Marshall stacks went on to be used by some of the greatest rock guitarists, including Jimi Hendrix, Jimmy Page and Eddie Van Halen. Marshall himself received the nickname "Lord of Loud." In the 1984 satirical movie "Spinal Tap," one character says his Marshall amplifier "goes to 11" (the volume knobs are conventionally marked 0-10). The amplifier and speakers in this display were extensively used at Get The Led Out concerts nationwide, including at the second Electric Factory in Philadelphia.

| On loan from Paul Edwin Hammond, Get The Led Out

FENDER STRATOCASTER
alder body, rosewood fingerboard
1969

After the success of the Telecaster in 1951, Leo Fender designed the "Strat" in 1954. In 1959, rosewood replaced maple on the fingerboard, and in 1968 polyurethane replaced the nitrocellulose body finish, as the latter tended to wear off. This instrument is an early example with the new finish. Although the neck was stamped by Fender in December 1968, other components used in the final assembly were stamped at the beginning of August 1969 (coincidentally during the same week that Electric Factory Concerts mounted the Atlantic City Pop Festival).

| Lent by R. Scott Hanson

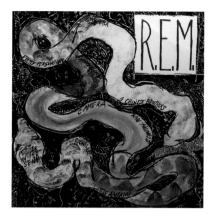

R.E.M. "RECKONING" (OR "FILE UNDER WATER") ALBUM COVER

Designed by Howard Finster & Michael Stipe, 1984
Georgia, United States

| On loan from R. Scott Hanson

CITY OF LOCALO GIBSON LES PAUL, 1991

Painted with colored paint and marker pens by Howard Finster (1916–2001), Summerville, GA, 1993

This Les Paul was painted by the preacher and outsider artist Howard Finster at his Paradise Garden, in Summerville, Georgia, on Oct. 26, 1993. Finster's vast output of paintings and objects became known to the museum-going public during the 1970s, and in the following decade he attracted the interest of musicians. Nearby Athens-based indie rock band R.E.M. used Paradise Garden as the setting for the music video accompanying their 1983 single "Radio Free Europe," and also for the cover of their second album "Reckoning" in 1984. Talking Heads recruited Finster to do the cover for their "Little Creatures" album in 1985. Finster is not known to have painted other guitars.

| On loan from R. Scott Hanson

Not Pictured

1967 CADILLAC COUPE DEVILLE

Painted by Benny Jimenez, Westphal College of Media Arts and Design, Drexel University

The original Electric Factory on Arch Street (1968–70) possessed an eye-catching 1959 Cadillac Coupe de Ville limousine, painted psychedelically by the same artists who decorated the venue's interior, including Rob "Ichabod" Stewart and Lisa Patch. This car is intended to capture the spirit of the original, which the Grateful Dead used to tour Philadelphia during their week playing Electric Factory in 1969.

High tailfins were a defining feature of American cars in the 1950s and early '60s, influencing other spheres of design. When Cream played at the Electric Factory in 1968, Eric Clapton visited a Philadelphia music store and purchased a Gibson Firebird guitar, whose raked shape was inspired by automobile tailfins.

SQUIER BY FENDER STRATOCASTER GUITAR
Given by Bob Dylan to Larry Magid, inscribed
"Best wishes, Thank (you)"

| On loan from Larry Magid

FENDER TELECASTER GUITAR
Given by Bruce Springsteen to Larry Magid,
inscribed "thanks Larry! Bruce Springsteen"

| On loan from Larry Magid

FENDER ELECTRIC MANDOLIN, 2008
Given by Levon Helm to Larry Magid, inscribed
"Levon Helm" and "Larry Campbell"

Larry Magid introduced the Levon Helm Band
when they played the second Electric Factory in
February 2008

| On loan from Larry Magid

ANNIE HASLAM, LEONARDO DA VINCI, PAINT
ON FENDER D'AQUISTO GUITAR
Given by Annie Haslam to Larry Magid

In common with a number of British rock
musicians who started out at art and design
schools, Annie Haslam studied fashion design
before becoming the lead singer of Renaissance in
1971. She has maintained a parallel career in the
visual arts.

| On loan from Larry Magid

VALLEY ARTS LIVE 8 GUITAR
Custom-built in the shape of the African
continent, African zebrawood body, inscribed on
the headstock "Live8 Philadelphia July 2, 2005"

| On loan from Larry Magid

BILL HALEY AND HIS COMETS, "ROCK AROUND THE CLOCK, " SHEET MUSIC

Max C. Freedman and Jimmy De Knight, 1953
Philadelphia, PA

After "Rock Around the Clock" featured on the soundtrack of "Blackboard Jungle," the 1955 movie about an inner-city school in New York, it topped the US chart and then the UK chart, becoming the first rock and roll song to do so. Recorded by Bill Haley and His Comets, who played in and around the Philadelphia area, "Rock Around the Clock" symbolized the initial wave of rejection of conventional values by American youth after World War II.

Its solo was played by Danny Cedrone, a highly regarded session guitarist who frequently played with Haley but also had his own band, the Esquire Boys. For the recording, he used his ES-300 equipped with a P-90 pickup, which had been introduced by Gibson that year and gave a warmer sound than its predecessors. Tragically, Cedrone died from a fall only two months after recording what would become one of the most influential solos in American rock music history.

The band — now Bill Haley and the Comets — played at the Spectrum on April 14, 1973 ("1st time In Philly in 15 years!") in a 1950's Rock & Roll Revival Concert that also featured Chuck Berry and Bo Diddley.

BIJOU CAFÉ T-SHIRT (BLUE & GREEN)
ca. 1972

| On loan from Special Collections and Research Center, Temple University

BRUCE SPRINGSTEEN TOUR SHIRT , 1978
Spectrum, Philadelphia, PA

| On loan from the Rock and Roll Hall of Fame and Museum

BIJOU CAFÉ T-SHIRT (BLUE) WITH ORIGINAL BIJOU LOGO
ca. 1972

| On loan from Special Collections and Research Center, Temple University

MEN'S POLYESTER LONG-SLEEVED BUTTON-DOWN SHIRT WITH OVERSIZED POINTED COLLAR.

Judd for Him, c. 1977
Gift of Howard Benson

Printed pattern on off-white ground having brown line drawings of castles around brown and purple mountains, with green-dotted orange clouds.

| On loan from the Robert & Penny Fox Historic Costume Collection

DYLAN
Poster designed by Milton Glaser, 1966, New York, NY, Offset lithograph

| On loan from R. Scott Hanson

69

TIME MAGAZINE, VOL. 90, NO. 1 "THE HIPPIES PHILOSOPHY OF A SUBCULTURE"
July 7, 1967

| On loan from R. Scott Hanson

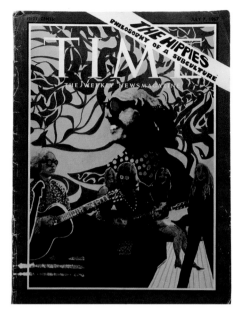

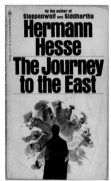

"ROSSHALDE"
Hermann Hesse, (1914), 1971

"THE JOURNEY TO THE EAST"
Hermann Hesse, (1932), 1972

"SIDDHARTHA"
Hermann Hesse, (1922), 1974

Among the more obvious influences on young people engaged in a "turn to the East," and a turn inwards, was the Nobel Prize-winning German novelist Herman Hesse, whose central characters invariably engage in spiritual struggle. These three covers date from the first half of the 1970s.

| On loan from Derek Gillman

PAUL MCCARTNEY AUTOGRAPHED WORLD TOUR PROGRAM
1989

These tour booklets were given to concert attendees free of charge and contained the tour itinerary, profiles on the band members, information on tour logistics, and the mission for Friends of the Earth.

| On loan from the Rock and Roll Hall of Fame and Museum

ROCK-OLA JUKEBOX, MODEL 448 ("MUSICAL MINT"), 1971–72

USA

Mechanical systems for what became known as jukeboxes increased in sophistication over the decades following the U.S. invention of a coin-operated phonograph in the late 19th century. Exteriors also developed, with manufacturing companies like Wurlizer, Seeburg and Rock-Ola competing in the use of often extravagant architectural elements and colored lighting.

After World War II, and the introduction of 45 rpm (revolutions per minute) records, jukeboxes became an expected fixture of diners, bars and pubs in America and Britain. During the 1950s and early '60s, jukeboxes were the principal means by which people would hear popular music in public spaces. Their presence was eroded by two factors: the first was the popularity in the 1960s of the portable transistor radio, which became a gift of choice for teenagers; the second was an increase in the appearance of major acts at stadium concerts, such as those produced by Electric Factory Concerts.

When the Chambers Brothers played the very first Electric Factory show, in February 1968, the sound came from two jukeboxes rigged at either side of the stage. The music in these two rooms is being provided from a pre-selected playlist on this Rock-Ola, with all the artists having performed at the original Electric Factory, or at Electric Factory Concerts shows, or both.

| On loan from Edward Zawora, '24

THE BEATLES "REVOLVER" ALBUM COVER
COVER DESIGNED BY KLAUS VOORMANN, 1966
London, England

| On loan from David & Leslie Clouser

THE BEATLES "SGT. PEPPER'S LONELY HEARTS CLUB BAND" ALBUM COVER
Cover designed by Jann Haworth and Peter Blake, 1967
London, England

The Beatles had a huge impact not only on music but also acted as a conduit for fashionable forms of art and design, delivering them to a wide audience. Klaus Voormann represented the Beatles in art nouveau style for "Revolver" after seeing an exhibition of the provocative Victorian illustrator Aubrey Beardsley at the Victoria and Albert Museum.

On the cover of "Sgt. Pepper's Lonely Hearts Club Band," designed by Pop artists Jann Haworth and Peter Blake, the Beatles adopt the current British street fashion for military parade uniforms. The versions they wear in "Sgt. Pepper" are more extravagant than actual uniforms, which were being recycled by the London boutique I was Lord Kitchener's Valet.

| On loan from Carolyn & Phil Fuhrman

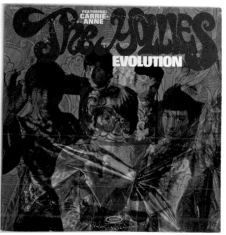

PROCOL HARUM "PROCOL HARUM" ALBUM COVER

Cover designed by Dickinson, 1967
England

Aubrey Beardsley's sinuous lines appealed to
designers in the 1960's and early 70's, when Art
Nouveau style and Symbolism came back into
fashion. Late 19th century Symbolist artists
and writers focused on the mythical, visionary
and dreamlike. The hallucinatory quality of
Beardsley's artwork resonated with psychedelic
imagery being created in California and London.

Beardsley's style was followed by German graphic
designer and Manfred Mann bassist Klaus
Voormann on the Beatle's 1966 Revolver cover,
and by the artist Dickinson on the 1967 Procol
Harum cover.

| On loan from Carolyn & Phil Fuhrman

IMI HENDRIX "ARE YOU EXPERIENCED" U.S. ALBUM COVER

Cover designed by Karl Ferris, 1967
London, England

| On loan from David & Leslie Clouser

THE HOLLIES "EVOLUTION" ALBUM COVER

Cover designed by Karl Ferris and Fool Collective
1967
London, England

Fool Collective was formed in London in 1967 by
Dutch psychedelic artist-designers Marijke Koger,
Simon Posthuma and Josje Leeger, together with
Leeger's partner Barry Finch. In preparation for
Cream's upcoming tours of Europe and the U.S.,
Fool designed stage clothes and painted Eric
Clapton's and Jack Bruce's guitars. The painted
Fender Bass VI is on display in the exhibition

Koger and Posthuma had been encouraged to
London by English photographer Karl Ferris
who then collaborated with Fool on the Hollies'
"Evolution" cover, and also designed the U.S. cover
for Jimi Hendrix's "Are You Experienced."

GRATEFUL DEAD "THE GRATEFUL DEAD"
Cover designed by Mouse Studios, 1967

| On loan from Carolyn & Phil Fuhrman

JEFFERSON AIRPLANE "AFTER BATHING AT BAXTER'S"
Cover designed by Ron Cobb, 1967

| On loan from Carolyn & Phil Fuhrman

CREAM "DISRAELI GEARS" ALBUM COVER
Cover designed by Martin Sharp, 1967
London, England

CREAM "WHEELS OF FIRE" ALBUM COVER
Cover designed by Martin Sharp, 1968
London, England

An important figure in late '60s psychedelic design
was Australian artist Martin Sharp, co-editor
of the Underground magazine Oz, published in
Sydney and London. Sharp's illustrations for Oz
parallel his covers for Cream's "Disraeli Gears"
and "Wheels of Fire."

GROVER WASHINGTON, JR. "LIVE AT THE BIJOU" ALBUM COVER
Designed by Bernie Block, 1977
Recorded May 1977
Bijou Café, Philadelphia, PA

2ND QUAKER CITY JAZZ FESTIVAL,
SEPT. 30 – OCT. 1, 1967
Spectrum, Philadelphia, PA

| On loan from Special Collections and Research Center,
Temple University

JIMI HENDRIX, 1968
Photo by J. Paul Simeone
Spectrum, Philadelphia, PA

| On loan from Larry Magid

ERIC CLAPTON, 1968
Photo by J. Paul Simeone
Electric Factory, Philadelphia, PA

| On loan from Larry Magid

ELECTRIC FACTORY POSTER FOR FIRST SHOWS, LISTING THE CHAMBERS BROS., FIRST BORNE, WOODYS TRUCK STOP, JIMI HENDRIX EXPERIENCE, AND OTHERS, FEB. 2–4, 1968
Electric Factory, Philadelphia, PA

| On loan from Special Collections and Research Center, Temple University

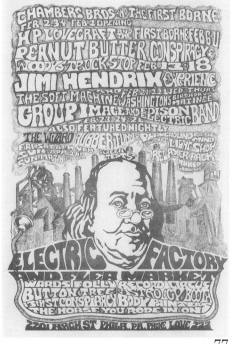

SEVEN PHOTOGRAPHS FROM THE ORIGINAL ELECTRIC FACTORY CONSTRUCTION, 1968

Behind-the-scenes photos of the painting and set-up of the original Electric Factory at 2201 Arch St., Philadelphia. Art student Lisa Patch from the Philadelphia Museum School (later incorporated into the University of the Arts) is seen painting on one of the columns.

| On loan from Special Collections and Research Center, Temple University

EXTERIOR OF ORIGINAL ELECTRIC FACTORY WITH BEN FRANKLIN SIGN, CA. 1968

Philadelphia, PA

| On loan from Special Collections and Research Center, Temple University

JIMI HENDRIX EXPERIENCE (REPRODUCTION OF POSTER), FEB. 21–22, 1968
Electric Factory, Philadelphia, PA

| On loan from Special Collections and Research Center, Temple University

BIG BROTHER AND THE HOLDING COMPANY, MARCH 15–17, 1968
Electric Factory, Philadelphia, PA

| On loan from Special Collections and Research Center, Temple University

CREAM AND WOODY'S TRUCK STOP, APRIL 12–14, 1968
Electric Factory, Philadelphia, PA

| On loan from Special Collections and Research Center, Temple University

DISTANT DRUMMER MAGAZINE, NO. 7, WITH ELECTRIC FACTORY AD, JUNE, 1968

Philadelphia, PA

| On loan from Special Collections and Research Center, Temple University

3RD ANNUAL QUAKER CITY JAZZ FESTIVAL, OCT. 20, 1968

Spectrum, Philadelphia, PA

| On loan from Special Collections and Research Center, Temple University

HISTORIC FAREWELL CONCERT: CREAM, NOV. 1, 1968

Spectrum, Philadelphia, PA

| On loan from Special Collections and Research Center, Temple University

ELECTRIC FACTORY MAGAZINE, PROOF, CA. 1969–1970

Philadelphia, PA

| On loan from Special Collections and Research Center, Temple University

**KODACOLOR PRINTS OF THE GRATEFUL DEAD
PERFORMING AT THE ELECTRIC FACTORY**
Photographs by Andrew Levinson, 1969

| On loan from Andrew J. Levinson

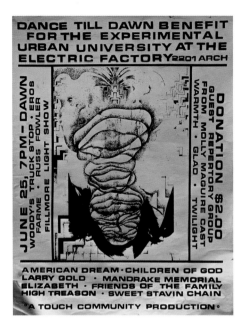

DANCE TILL DAWN BENEFIT FOR THE EXPERIMENTAL URBAN UNIVERSITY AT THE ELECTRIC FACTORY, JUNE 25, 1969
Electric Factory, Philadelphia, PA

| On loan from Special Collections and Research Center, Temple University

ATLANTIC CITY POP FESTIVAL (REPRODUCTION OF POSTER), AUG. 1–3, 1969
Atlantic City Racetrack, Atlantic City, NJ

| On loan from Special Collections and Research Center, Temple University

DARYL HALL AND JOHN OATES WITH LARRY MAGID
Photo by John David Kalodner, ca. 1970

| On loan from Special Collections and Research Center, Temple University

" Led Zeppelin "   © J. Paul Simeone

LED ZEPPELIN, 1970
Photo by J. Paul Simeone
Spectrum, Philadelphia, PA

| On loan from Larry Magid

ELECTRIC FACTORY CONCERTS BOOGIE WOLF LOGO DESIGN, CA. 1970S
Philadelphia, PA

| On loan from Larry Magid

THE KINKS, JAN. 30-31, 1970
Electric Factory, Philadelphia, PA

| On loan from Special Collections and Research Center, Temple University

DELANEY, BONNIE & FRIENDS WITH ERIC CLAPTON, FEB. 11, 1970
Electric Factory, Philadelphia, PA

| On loan from Special Collections and Research Center, Temple University

IRON BUTTERFLY, FEB. 14, 1970
Spectrum, Philadelphia, PA

| On loan from Special Collections and Research Center, Temple University

CHICAGO, FEB. 20, 1970
McGonigle Hall, Temple University, Philadelphia, PA

| On loan from Special Collections and Research Center, Temple University

MANFRED MANN CHAPTER THREE (III), MAY 8-9, 1970
Electric Factory, Philadelphia, PA

| On loan from Special Collections and Research Center, Temple University

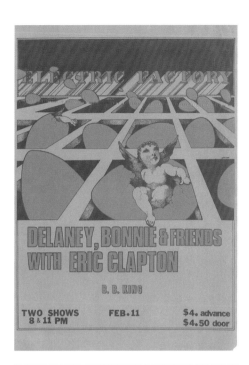

ELECTRIC FACTORY

DELANEY, BONNIE & FRIENDS
WITH ERIC CLAPTON

B. B. KING

TWO SHOWS   FEB. 11 $4. advance
8 & 11 PM $4.50 door

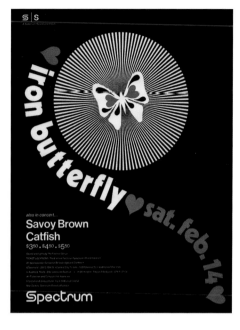

iron butterfly ♥ sat. feb. 14

also in concert...
Savoy Brown
Catfish
$3.50, $4.50, $5.50

Spectrum

Chicago

good news

FRIDAY FEB 20
BLOODGOOD HALL

MANFRED
MANN
CHAPTER III
MYLON
BLODWYN·PIG
MAY 8&9
ELECTRIC FACTORY
$3.50

NEIL YOUNG BACKSTAGE AT ELECTRIC FACTORY, FEB. 28, 1970

Photograph by Joel Berstein, Philadelphia, PA

| On loan from Special Collections and Research Center, Temple University

AUDIENCE AT THE SPECTRUM, 1973
Photograph by Joel Berstein, Philadelphia, PA

This photograph was used on the cover of Neil Young's "Time Fades Away" album, recorded live during his early 1973 tour.

| On loan from Special Collections and Research Center, Temple University

THE WHO, JUNE 24, 1970

Electric Factory Concerts
Spectrum, Philadelphia, PA

| On loan from Special Collections and Research Center,
Temple University

HARMONYVILLE, PLANNED FOR AUG. 4–9, 1970

With the acts already booked, this festival was
canceled after protests from local residents.
Walpack Center, New Jersey

| On loan from Special Collections and Research Center,
Temple University

DANCE CONCERT: THREE DOG NIGHT, JULY 24, 1970

Poster designed by Spencer Zahn
Spectrum, Philadelphia, PA

| On loan from Special Collections and Research Center,
Temple University

CHICAGO, AUG. 12, 1970
Photo by John David Kalodner
Spectrum, Philadelphia, PA

| On loan from Special Collections and Research Center,
Temple University

QUAKER CITY ROCK: GRAND FUNK RAILROAD, SMALL FACES WITH ROD STEWART, ERIC BURDON AND WAR, OCT. 23, 1970
Poster designed by Spencer Zahn
Spectrum, Philadelphia, PA

| On loan from Special Collections and Research Center,
Temple University

THE FIFTH DIMENSION, AUG. 25, 1970
Spectrum, Philadelphia, PA

| On loan from Special Collections and Research Center,
Temple University

ISAAC HAYES, OCT. 25, 1970
Spectrum, Philadelphia, PA

| On loan from Special Collections and Research Center,
Temple University

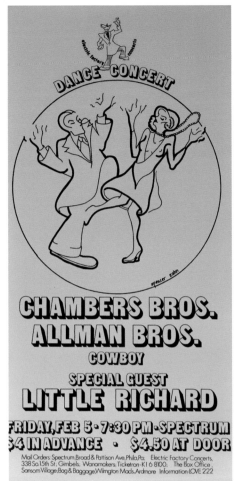

TEN YEARS AFTER, PROCOL HARUM, LEON RUSSELL, NOV. 14, 1970

Spectrum, Philadelphia, PA

| On loan from Special Collections and Research Center, Temple University

DANCE CONCERT: CHAMBERS BROS., ALLMAN BROS., FEB. 5, 1971

Spectrum, Philadelphia, PA

| On loan from Special Collections and Research Center, Temple University

RICHIE HAVENS AND THE YOUNGBLOODS, MARCH 7, 1971
Poster designed by Saban
Spectrum, Philadelphia, PA

| On loan from Special Collections and Research Center, Temple University

QUAKER CITY JAZZ, WITH NINA SIMONE AND OTHERS, SEPT. 19, 1971
Spectrum, Philadelphia, PA

| On loan from Special Collections and Research Center, Temple University

JOHN SEBASTIAN, CAPTAIN BEEFHEART & HIS MAGIC BAND, DEC. 12, 1970
Spectrum, Philadelphia, PA

| On loan from Special Collections and Research Center, Temple University

HOT TUNA, OCT. 1, 1971
Poster designed by Spencer Zahn
Spectrum, Philadelphia, PA

| On loan from Special Collections and Research Center, Temple University

LETTER (REPRODUCTION) ABOUT THE CLOSING OF THE ORIGINAL ELECTRIC FACTORY AT 2201 ARCH ST.,

Electric Factory Staff, 1971

| On loan from Special Collections and Research Center, Temple University

NEWSPAPER CLIPPING ABOUT THE OPENING OF BIJOU CAFÉ AT 1409 LOMBARD ST.

1972

Philadelphia, PA

| On loan from Special Collections and Research Center, Temple University

DAN HICKS & HIS HOT LICKS PERFORMING AT THE OPENING OF BIJOU CAFÉ

Oct. 4, 1972

Philadelphia, PA

| On loan from Special Collections and Research Center, Temple University

ORIGINAL BIJOU CAFÉ LOGO

1972

Philadelphia, PA

| On loan from Special Collections and Research Center, Temple University

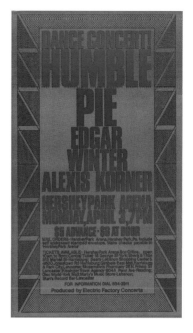

"ELECTRIC FACTORY CONCERTS 5", CONCERT MAGAZINE, VOL. 2, NO. 2, ANNIVERSARY ISSUE
ca. 1972
Philadelphia, PA

| On loan from Larry Magid

DANCE CONCERT!: HUMBLE PIE, EDGAR WINTER, ALEXIS KORNER, APRIL 3, 1972
Poster designed by Spencer Zahn
Hershey Park, Arena, Hershey, PA

| On loan from Special Collections and Research Center, Temple University

ROD STEWART, JULY 2, 1972
Spectrum, Philadelphia, PA

| On loan from Special Collections and Research Center, Temple University

BIJOU CAFÉ AD: "THE FINEST IN CONTEMPORARY ENTERTAINMENT GOOD DRINKS TOO!," CA. 1973
Philadelphia, PA

| On loan from Special Collections and Research Center, Temple University

NEW RIDERS OF THE PURPLE SAGE, APRIL 7, 1973
McGonigle Hall, Temple Campus, Philadelphia, PA

| On loan from Special Collections and Research Center, Temple University

PAUL BUTTERFIELD BETTER DAYS IN CONCERT, APRIL 20, 1973
Tower Theater, Philadelphia, PA

| On loan from Special Collections and Research Center, Temple University

GRATEFUL DEAD AND ALLMAN BROTHERS, JUNE 9–10, 1973
Electric Factory Concerts
R.F.K. Memorial Stadium, Washington, DC

| On loan from Special Collections and Research Center, Temple University

GRATEFUL DEAD, SEPT. 20–21, 1973
Spectrum, Philadelphia, PA

Jerry Garcia is playing his "Alligator" Stratocaster,
used from 1971–73.

| On loan from Special Collections and Research Center,
Temple University

JIM CROCE WITH MAURY MUEHLEISEN
Sept. 20, 1973, before fatal plane crash
Natchitoches, LA

| On loan from Special Collections and Research Center, Temple University

BOB DYLAN, JAN. 6–7, 1974
Spectrum, Philadelphia, PA

| On loan from Special Collections and Research Center, Temple University

RICHARD PRYOR AT BIJOU CAFÉ, AUG. 8, 1974
Bijou Café, Philadelphia, PA

| On loan from Larry Magid

BILLY JOEL, SEPT. 24–28, 1974
Photo by Zohrab Kazanjian, 1974
Bijou Café, Philadelphia, PA

| On loan from Special Collections and Research Center,
Temple University

ELTON JOHN, DEC. 2–3, 1974
Photo by Zohrab Kazanjian,
Spectrum, Philadelphia, PA

| On loan from Special Collections and Research Center,
Temple University

ALLEN SPIVAK AND LARRY MAGID, CA. 1975

| On loan from Larry Magid

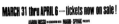

BETTE MIDLER'S ★

★ CLAMS
ON·THE·HALF·
SHELL REVUE ★

STARRING BETTE MIDLER GUEST STAR LIONEL HAMPTON DIRECTOR JOE LAYTON SETS & COSTUMES TONY WALTON

ERLANGER THEATER, 21st & Market Sts. (215) 561-5054
PREVIEWS! – PRIOR TO N.Y. ENGAGEMENT

Epic Records and Electric Factory Concerts
invite you to a
Silver Sin and Soul
Cocktail Party
in honor of
"LABELLE"
Tuesday, April 8th, 1975
11:30 p. m.
at
The Bijou Cafe
1409 Lombard Street
Philadelphia, Pennsylvania
This pass will admit one.

**BETTE MIDLER'S "CLAMS ON THE HALF SHELL" REVUE,
MARCH 31–APRIL 6, 1975**

Erlanger Theater, Philadelphia, PA

| On loan from Special Collections and Research Center,
Temple University

BONNIE RAITT, MID-1970S

Bijou Café, Philadelphia, PA

| On loan from Special Collections and Research Center,
Temple University

**EPIC RECORDS AND ELECTRIC FACTORY CONCERTS
INVITATION "LABELLE" (REPRODUCTION)**

Aachen Printing Company, 1975
Philadelphia, PA

| Courtesy of the Atwater Kent Collection, Drexel University

FREDDIE MERCURY FRONTING QUEEN, AUG. 12, 1975
Spectrum, Philadelphia, PA

| On loan from Special Collections and Research Center, Temple University

BOB MARLEY AT BIJOU CAFÉ, 1975
Bijou Café, Philadelphia, PA

| On loan from Special Collections and Research Center, Temple University

PATTI SMITH, DEC. 17–20, 1975
Bijou Café, Philadelphia, PA

| On loan from Special Collections and Research Center, Temple University

BRUCE SPRINGSTEEN, OCT. 25 OR 27, 1976
Spectrum, Philadelphia, PA

| On loan from Special Collections and Research Center, Temple University

JONI MITCHELL, FEB. 16, 1976
Spectrum, Philadelphia, PA

| On loan from Special Collections and Research Center, Temple University

DAVID BOWIE (AS "THIN WHITE DUKE"), MARCH 15, 1976
Spectrum, Philadelphia, PA

| On loan from Special Collections and Research Center, Temple University

KENN KWEDER AND HIS SECRET KIDS, FEB. 14–15, 1977
Photograph by Phil Ceccola
Bijou Café, Philadelphia, PA

| On loan from Special Collections and Research Center, Temple University

101

JERRY GARCIA, CA. 1977–79
Spectrum, Philadelphia, PA

| On loan from Special Collections and Research Center,
Temple University

BIJOU CAFÉ AD CARD FOR APRIL THROUGH MAY, 1980
Philadelphia, PA

| On loan from Special Collections and Research Center,
Temple University

ALLMAN BROTHERS, "THE ROUND UP," JUNE 20, 1981
JFK Stadium, Philadelphia, PA

| On loan from Special Collections and Research Center,
Temple University

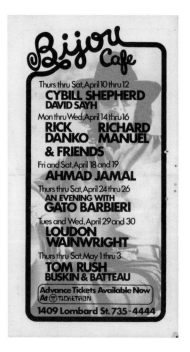

FOREIGNER, KINKS, JOAN JETT & THE BLACKHEARTS, LOVERBOY, HUEY LEWIS & THE NEWS, JUNE 19, 1982
JFK Stadium, Philadelphia, PA

| On loan from Special Collections and Research Center, Temple University

B.B. KING, MILLIE JACKSON, BOBBY "BLUE" BLAND, MARCH 19, 1983
Shubert Theater, Philadelphia, PA

| On loan from Special Collections and Research Center, Temple University

MARVIN GAYE, JULY 9, 1983
Spectrum, Philadelphia, PA

| On loan from Special Collections and Research Center, Temple University

PATTI LABELLE "I'M IN LOVE AGAIN" GOLD RECORD PRESENTED TO LARRY MAGID
1984
Philadelphia, PA

| On loan from Kaisha Blackstone

ELECTRIC FACTORY CONCERTS PRESENTS, OCTOBER 1984
Tower Theater, Philadelphia, PA

| On loan from Special Collections and Research Center, Temple University

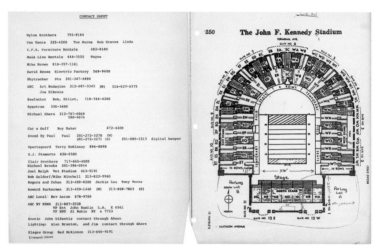

LIVE AID: JFK STADIUM SCHEMATICS AND CONTACT SHEET
1985
Philadelphia, PA

| On loan from Larry Magid

LIVE AID BOMBER JACKET
Satin Jackets, Inc., 1985

| On loan from Hard Rock International

LIVE AID MENU
1985

| On loan from Hard Rock International

"WE ARE THE WORLD" ALBUM COVER
Cover designed by John Lykes & Rolan Young,
1985
New York, NY

| On loan from Ed Zawora

LIVE AID CONCERT MAGAZINE
1985
Philadelphia, PA

| On loan from Larry Magid

HOT AIR BALLOON AT LIVE AID, JULY 13, 1985
JFK Stadium, Philadelphia, PA
Photograph by Ken Regan

| On loan from Special Collections and Research Center,
Temple University

LIVE AID LOGO DESIGNS
1985
Philadelphia, PA

| On loan from Larry Magid

LIVE AID FLYER AND TICKET
1985
Philadelphia, PA

| On loan from Larry Magid

CANDID PHOTOGRAPH OF LIVE AID CROWD, JULY 13, 1985
JFK Stadium, Philadelphia, PA

| On loan from Larry Magid

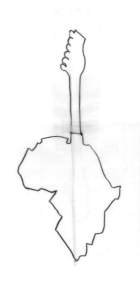

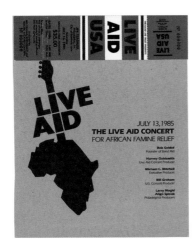

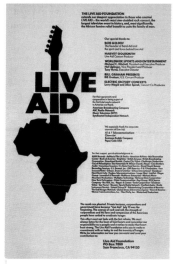

LIVE AID CROWD AND STAGE, JULY 13, 1985
Photograph by Ken Regan
JFK Stadium, Philadelphia, PA

| On loan from Larry Magid

LARRY BACKSTAGE AT LIVE AID, JULY 13, 1985
JFK Stadium, Philadelphia, PA

| On loan from Larry Magid

LIVE AID TICKETS
1985
JFK Stadium, Philadelphia, PA

| On loan from Andy McFadden

LIVE AID "THANK YOU" PIECE IN THE WALL STREET JOURNAL, JULY 19, 1985
Live Aid Foundation
Philadelphia, PA

| On loan from Larry Magid

GROUP PHOTOGRAPH OF PERFORMERS AT LIVE AID, JULY 13, 1985
Photograph by Ken Regan
JFK Stadium, Philadelphia, PA
| On loan from Special Collections and Research Center, Temple University

BOB DYLAN, KEITH RICHARDS AND RONNIE WOOD PERFORMING AT LIVE AID, JULY 13, 1985
Photograph by Ken Regan
JFK Stadium, Philadelphia, PA

| On loan from Special Collections and Research Center, Temple University

RUN-D.M.C. PERFORMING AT LIVE AID, JULY 13, 1985
Photograph by Ken Regan
JFK Stadium, Philadelphia, PA

| On loan from Special Collections and Research Center, Temple University

ERIC CLAPTON PERFORMING AT LIVE AID, JULY 13, 1985
J Photograph by Ken Regan
FK Stadium, Philadelphia, PA

| On loan from Special Collections and Research Center, Temple University

TOM PETTY & THE HEARTBREAKERS PERFORMING AT LIVE AID, JULY 13, 1985
J Photograph by Ken Regan
FK Stadium, Philadelphia, PA

| On loan from Special Collections and Research Center, Temple University

MICK JAGGER AND TINA TURNER PERFORMING AT LIVE AID, JULY 13, 1985
Photograph by Ken Regan
JFK Stadium, Philadelphia, PA

| On loan from Special Collections and Research Center, Temple University

THE FOUR TOPS PERFORMING AT LIVE AID, JULY 13, 1985
Photograph by Ken Regan
JFK Stadium, Philadelphia, PA

| On loan from Special Collections and Research Center, Temple University

MADONNA PERFORMING AT LIVE AID, JULY 13, 1985
Photograph by Ken Regan
JFK Stadium, Philadelphia, PA

| On loan from Special Collections and Research Center, Temple University

GEORGE THOROGOOD AND ALBERT COLLINS PERFORMING AT LIVE AID, JULY 13, 1985
Photograph by Ken Regan
JFK Stadium, Philadelphia, PA

| On loan from Special Collections and Research Center, Temple University

PATTI LABELLE PERFORMING AT LIVE AID, JULY 13, 1985
Photograph by Ken Regan
JFK Stadium, Philadelphia, PA

| On loan from Special Collections and Research Center, Temple University

PHIL COLLINS PERFORMING AT LIVE AID,
JULY 13, 1985
Photograph by Ken Regan
JFK Stadium, Philadelphia, PA

| On loan from Special Collections and Research Center, Temple University

THE BEACH BOYS PERFORMING AT LIVE AID,
JULY 13, 1985
Photograph by Ken Regan
JFK Stadium, Philadelphia, PA

| On loan from Special Collections and Research Center, Temple University

OZZY OSBOURNE PERFORMING AT LIVE AID,
JULY 13, 1985
Photograph by Ken Regan
JFK Stadium, Philadelphia, PA

| On loan from Special Collections and Research Center, Temple University

MIKE D. OF BEASTIE BOYS, AUG. 16, 1987
Spectrum, Philadelphia, PA

| On loan from Special Collections and Research Center, Temple University

BON JOVI, NEW JERSEY SYNDICATE TOUR, JUNE 19–20, 1989
Spectrum, Philadelphia, PA

| On loan from Special Collections and Research Center, Temple University

STEVIE NICKS, THE WHOLE LOTTA TROUBLE TOUR, JULY 26, 1991
Spectrum, Philadelphia, PA

| On loan from Special Collections and Research Center, Temple University

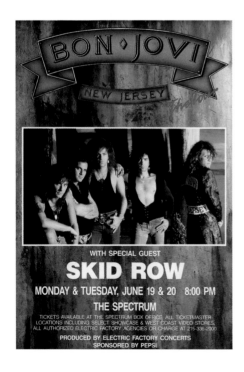

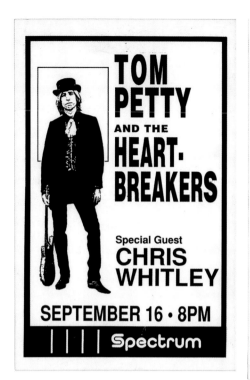

TOM PETTY AND THE HEARTBREAKERS, SEPTEMBER 16, 1991

Spectrum, Philadelphia, PA

| On loan from Special Collections and Research Center, Temple University

GEORGE MICHAEL, COVER TO COVER TOUR, OCT. 29, 1991

Spectrum, Philadelphia, PA

| On loan from Special Collections and Research Center, Temple University

PETER GABRIEL, JULY 6, 1993

Spectrum, Philadelphia, PA

| On loan from Special Collections and Research Center, Temple University

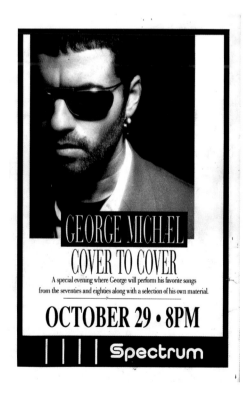

THE MOODY BLUES, JULY 8, 1993
Taj Mahal, Atlantic City, NJ

| On loan from Special Collections and Research Center, Temple University

GRATEFUL DEAD, SEPT. 12–14, 1993
Spectrum, Philadelphia, PA

| On loan from Special Collections and Research Center, Temple University

PLAQUE PRESENTED TO LARRY MAGID FOR INAUGURAL CONCERT AT CORESTATES SPECTRUM WITH OASIS
Sept. 2, 1996

| On loan from Special Collections and Research Center, Temple University

B.B. KING, BOBBY "BLUE" BLAND, APRIL 11, 1999
Tower Theater, Philadelphia, PA

| On loan from Special Collections and Research Center, Temple University

GO-GO'S AND B-52'S, JULY 17, 2000
E-Centre, Camden, NJ

| On loan from Special Collections and Research Center, Temple University

BOB DYLAN AND PHIL LESH, JULY 28, 2000
Poster designed by Christopher Peterson

E-Centre, Camden, NJ

| On loan from Special Collections and Research Center, Temple University

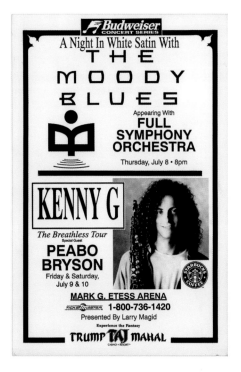

Electric Factory Proudly Presents An Evening With

The King of the Blues

B.B.
KING

and his Very Special Guest

Bobby 'Blue'
BLAND

Sunday · April 11 · 1999

The
Tower Theater
Philadelphia

8:00 PM · The Tower Theater · 69th and Ludlow in Upper Darby
Tickets Available at the TLA Box Office · Ticketmaster Locations · Charge: 215-336-2000
For Information on all Electric Factory Shows call: 215-LOVE-222 · www.electricfactory.com

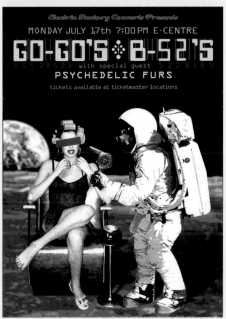

Electric Factory Concerts Presents

MONDAY JULY 17th 7:00 PM E-CENTRE

GO-GO'S ✧ B-52'S

with special guest

PSYCHEDELIC FURS

tickets available at ticketmaster locations

Electric Factory Concerts Presents

Bob
Dylan
Phil
Lesh

E•Centre
July 28th 7pm

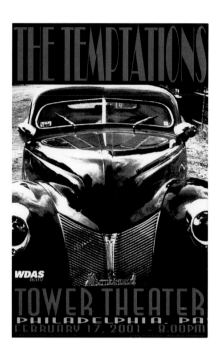

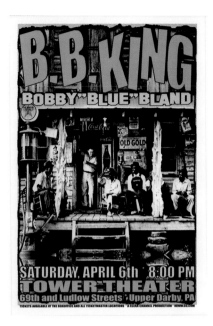

THE TEMPTATIONS, FEB. 17, 2001
Tower Theater, Philadelphia, PA

| On loan from Special Collections and Research Center,
Temple University

B.B. KING AND BOBBY "BLUE" BLAND, APRIL 6, 2002
Tower Theater, Philadelphia, PA

| On loan from Special Collections and Research Center,
Temple University

AEROSMITH, KID ROCK AND RUN D.M.C., SEPT. 7, 2002
Tweeter Center, Camden, NJ

| On loan from Special Collections and Research Center,
Temple University

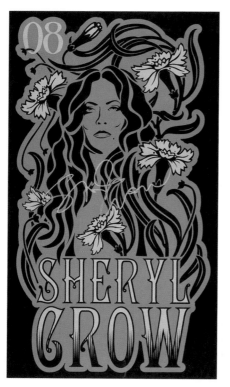

KING CRIMSON, MARCH 7, 2003
Tower Theater, Philadelphia, PA

| On loan from Larry Magid

NORAH JONES AND THE HANDSOME BAND,
APRIL 20, 2007
Tower Theater, Philadelphia, PA

| On loan from Special Collections and Research Center,
Temple University

SHERYL CROW, SIGNED POSTER, CA. 2009
Philadelphia, PA

| On loan from Special Collections and Research Center,
Temple University

LARRY MAGID AND HERB SPIVAK, 2018
Photograph by Dallyn Pavey

| On loan from Larry Magid

HOLE, JUNE 22, 2010
Poster designed by J. P. Flexner
Electric Factory, Philadelphia, PA

| On loan from Graphic Design, URBN Center, Drexel
University

CITIZEN COPE, OCT. 27, 2012
Poster designed by Max Gordon
Electric Factory, Philadelphia, PA

| On loan from Graphic Design, URBN Center, Drexel
University

MINUS THE BEAR, OCT. 15, 2011
Poster designed by Max Gordon
Electric Factory, Philadelphia, PA

| On loan from Graphic Design, URBN Center, Drexel
University

GROUP LOVE, NOV. 1, 2012
Poster designed by Ralph Stollenwerk
Electric Factory, Philadelphia, PA

| On loan from Special Collections and Research Center,
Temple University

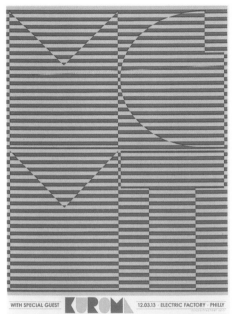

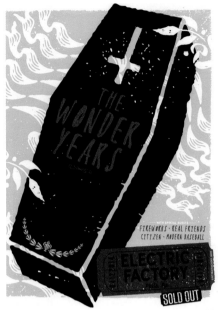

MGMT, DEC. 3, 2013
Poster designed by Ralph Stollenwerk
Electric Factory, Philadelphia, PA

| On loan from Special Collections and Research Center,
Temple University

MATT & KIM, APRIL 17, 2015
Poster designed by Ralph Stollenwerk
Electric Factory, Philadelphia, PA

| On loan from Graphic Design, URBN Center, Drexel
University

THE WONDER YEARS, APRIL 12, 2014
Poster designed by Ralph Stollenwerk
Electric Factory, Philadelphia, PA

| On loan from Special Collections and Research Center,
Temple University

THE STORY SO FAR, MAY 23, 2015
Electric Factory, Philadelphia, PA

| On loan from Special Collections and Research Center,
Temple University

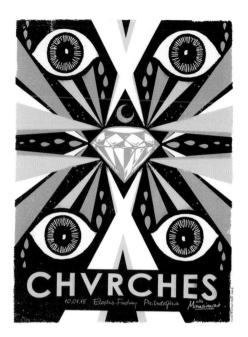

CHVRCHES, OCT. 1, 2015
Poster designed by Ralph Stollenwerk
Electric Factory, Philadelphia, PA

| On loan from Special Collections and Research Center, Temple University

NERO, OCT. 14, 2015
Poster designed by Ralph Stollenwerk
Electric Factory, Philadelphia, PA

| On loan from Graphic Design, URBN Center, Drexel University

THE NEIGHBORHOOD, OCT. 6, 2015
Electric Factory, Philadelphia, PA

| On loan from Graphic Design, URBN Center, Drexel University

CIRCA SURVIVE, NOV. 27, 2015
Poster designed by Ralph Stollenwerk
Electric Factory, Philadelphia, PA

| On loan from Graphic Design, URBN Center, Drexel University

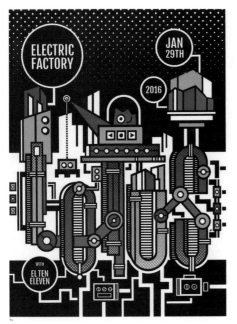

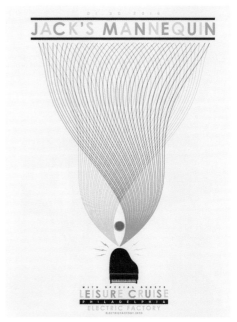

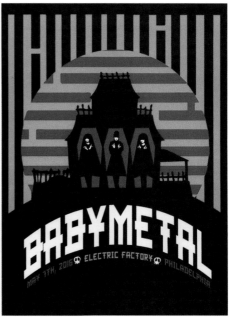

LOTUS, JAN. 29, 2016
Electric Factory, Philadelphia, PA

| On loan from Graphic Design, URBN Center, Drexel
University

DROPKICK MURPHY'S, MARCH 13, 2016
Poster designed by Max Gordon
Electric Factory, Philadelphia, PA

| On loan from Graphic Design, URBN Center, Drexel
University

JACK'S MANNEQUIN, JAN. 30, 2016
Poster designed by Ralph Stollenwerk
Electric Factory, Philadelphia, PA

| On loan from Graphic Design, URBN Center, Drexel
University

BABY METAL, MAY 7, 2016
Electric Factory, Philadelphia, PA

| On loan from Special Collections and Research Center,
Temple University

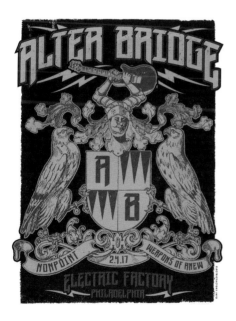

COURTNEY BARNETT, MAY 26, 2016
Poster designed by Eric Hinkley
Electric Factory, Philadelphia, PA

| On loan from Graphic Design, URBN Center, Drexel
University

ALTER BRIDGE, FEB. 4, 2017
Poster designed by Ralph Stollenwerk
Electric Factory, Philadelphia, PA

| On loan from Graphic Design, URBN Center, Drexel
University

ZED'S DEAD, OCT. 1, 2016
Poster designed by Max Gordon
Electric Factory, Philadelphia, PA

| On loan from Graphic Design, URBN Center, Drexel
University

BANKS, JUNE 2, 2017
Electric Factory, Philadelphia, PA

| On loan from Graphic Design, URBN Center, Drexel University

BANOBO WITH ROMERE, APRIL 29, 2017
Poster designed by Tracy Feldman
Electric Factory, Philadelphia, PA

| On loan from Graphic Design, URBN Center, Drexel University

NINJA SEX PARTY AUG. 27-28, 2017
Electric Factory, Philadelphia, PA

| On loan from Graphic Design, URBN Center, Drexel University

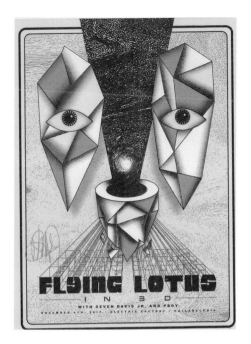

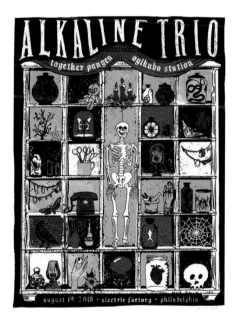

FLYING LOTUS, NOV. 4, 2017
Electric Factory, Philadelphia, PA

| On loan from Graphic Design, URBN Center, Drexel
University

ALKALINE TRIO, AUG. 19, 2018
Poster designed by Tracy Feldman
Electric Factory, Philadelphia, PA

| On loan from Graphic Design, URBN Center, Drexel
University

ST. VINCENT, NOV. 28, 2017
Poster designed by Tracy Feldman
Electric Factory, Philadelphia, PA

| On loan from Special Collections and Research Center,
Temple University

127

IMAGE CREDITS

POLITICS IN THE 1960S

Fig. 1: Signs carried by many marchers during the March on Washington in 1963.
| Library of Congress, Prints & Photographs Division, photography by Marion S. Trikosko [reproduction number, e.g., LC-DIG-ppmsca-37245]

Fig. 2: "Crowds mill about after all-night rioting in North Philadelphia. Firemen are at the scene to battle blaze in a store at 1510 West Columbia Avenue" from the Philadelphia Evening Bulletin covering the Columbia Avenue riots Aug. 29, 1964.
| Philadelphia Evening Bulletin. George D. McDowell Philadelphia Evening Bulletin Collection. Special Collections Research Center, Temple University Libraries, Philadelphia, PA.

Fig 3: A Department of Defense high altitude aerial reconnaissance photograph of medium-range ballistic missile (MRBM) launch site number 1 in San Cristobal, Cuba on Oct. 14, 1962.
| United States. Department of Defense. Department of Defense Cuban Missile Crisis Briefing Materials. John F. Kennedy Presidential Library and Museum, Boston.

Fig. 4: Excerpt from "The Port Huron Statement" by the Students for a Democratic Society, June 15, 1962.
| Students for a Democratic Society. "The Port Huron Statement". Public Paper, December 31, 1962. From Teaching American History. https://teachingamericanhistory.org/document/port-huron-statement/ (accessed June 8, 2023).

Fig. 5: Inauguration of President John F. Kennedy on the East Portico of the U.S. Capitol on Jan. 20, 1961.
| Architect of the Capitol photo courtesy of the Library of Congress, Prints & Photographs Division, Reproduction number e.g., LC-USZ62-12345]

Fig. 6: Trip to Texas: Swearing-in ceremony aboard Air Force One as Lyndon B. Johnson (LBJ) became President on Nov. 22, 1963.
| Photo by Cecil Stoughton. White House Photographs. John F. Kennedy Presidential Library and Museum, Boston.

Fig. 7: Secretary of Defense Robert McNamara pointing to a map of Vietnam at a press conference in 1965.
| Library of Congress, Prints & Photographs Division, photography by Marion S. Trikosko [reproduction number, e.g., LC-USZ62-134155].

Fig. 8: Black Panther Convention, Lincoln Memorial in 1970.
| Library of Congress, Prints & Photographs Division, photography by Thomas J. O'Halloran and Warren K. Leffler [reproduction number, e.g., LC-U9-22860-27]

CULTURAL REVOLUTION

Fig. 1: Cover of "Siddhartha" by Herman Hesse, which was published in 1922 and became an influential novel in the United States in the 1960s.

| Hesse, Herman. Siddhartha. United States: New Directions, 1951.

Fig. 2: Ravi Shankar with his student George Harrison in Los Angeles, CA in 1967.
| © John Malmin, March 28, 1971, Los Angeles Times Photographic Collection, University of California, Los Angeles, Library. Department of Special Collections, https://digital.library.ucla.edu/
catalog/ark:/21198/zz0002w617, Attribution 4.0 International

THE ELECTRIC GUITAR

Fig. 1: Bruce Springsteen, August 14–15, 1985, JFK Stadium, Philadelphia, PA
| Photo by Zohrab Kazanjian, 1985, Special Collections and Research Center, Temple University

Fig. 2: Jimmy Page of Led Zeppelin playing a Les Paul at the Spectrum, 1970.
| Photo © J. Paul Simeone

ELECTRIC FACTORY

Fig. 1: Lisa Patch from the Museum School (now the University of the Arts) helped paint the original Electric Factory warehouse with psychedelic designs both inside and out.
|Special Collections Research Center, Temple University Libraries, Philadelphia, PA

Fig. 2: A 1959 Cadillac limousine with a psychedelic paint job sat outside the original Electric Factory.
|Photo © Lewis Bernstein, circa 1969

Fig. 3: Early photographs of the interior of original Electric Factory warehouse.
|Special Collections Research Center, Temple University Libraries, Philadelphia, PA

Fig. 4: Eric Clapton as a member of Cream, at Electric Factory, April 1968, playing a Gibson Firebird guitar that he had just purchased from a music store in Philadelphia.
|Photo © J. Paul Simeone 2005, Collection of Larry Magid

Fig. 5: Jerry Garcia and Mickey Hart of the Grateful Dead backstage at Electric Factory, February 1969
|Photo by Andrew Levinson, 1969

Fig. 6: Grateful Dead playing at Electric Factory, February 1969
|Photo by Andrew Levinson, 1969

ELECTRIC FACTORY CONCERTS

Fig. 1: Interior of the Bijou Café on opening night with Dan Hicks & His Hot Licks performing, 1972.
|Special Collections Research Center, Temple University Libraries, Philadelphia, PA.

Fig. 2: The Chambers Brothers performing at the Spectrum for the 1st Quaker City Rock Festival in Philadelphia on Oct. 19, 1968
| The Chambers Brothers, 1968, ©Ron Karr Photography

Fig. 3: The article "Bijou Café Caters to 'Hip' Crowd" on the opening night of the Bijou Café on Oct. 4, 1972 with headliner Dan Hicks & His Hot Licks.
| Special Collections Research Center, Temple University Libraries, Philadelphia, PA.

Fig. 4: Richard Pryor performing at the Bijou Café, 1974.
|Collection of Larry Magid

ATLANTIC CITY POP FESTIVAL

Fig. 1: Procol Harum performing songs from the album "A Salty Dog" at the Atlantic City Pop Festival in 1969.
|Procol Harum, 1969, Ron Karr, ©Ron Karr Photography

Fig. 2: Poster for Atlantic City Pop Festival, Aug. 1–3, 1969.
|Special Collections Research Center, Temple University Libraries, Philadelphia, PA

Fig. 3: Janis Joplin performing at the Atlantic City Pop Festival in 1969.
|Janis Joplin, 1969, Ron Karr, ©Ron Karr Photography

RHYTHM, BEAT AND THE INFLUENCE OF AFRICA

Fig. 1: Publicity photo of the American band Sly and the Family Stone in 1968.
| Distributed by Epic Records, Daedalus Management, and William Morris Agency, Inc., Photographer uncredited and unknown.

Fig. 2: Bob Marley performing at the Bijou Café Nov. 10–11, 1975.
|Special Collections Research Center, Temple University Libraries, Philadelphia, PA.

Fig. 3: Congo Square in New Orleans served as a place where enslaved and free African Americans congregated.
| The Bamboula, March 1886, Edward Windsor Kemble, The Historic New Orleans Collection, 1974.25.23.54

129

LIVE AID

Fig. 1: Image of the hot air balloon at Live Aid, July 13, 1985.
| Photo by Ken Regan, Special Collections Research Center, Temple University Libraries, Philadelphia, PA.

Fig. 2: Ad expressing appreciation to those who created Live Aid in The Wall Street Journal, Friday, July 19, 1985.
| Special Collections Research Center, Temple University Libraries, Philadelphia, PA.

Fig. 3: Aerial view of the Live Aid crowd in JFK Stadium on July 13, 1985.
| Photo by Ken Regan, Special Collections Research Center, Temple University Libraries, Philadelphia, PA.

CLAIR SOUND SYSTEMS

Fig. 1: Clair Bros. Custom Console / "The Elvis Board," ca. 1971
| Photo by Mary Elizabeth Kulesa, 2023. Courtesy of Clair Global.

Fig. 2: SAE Mark II Amplifier, ca 1967
| Photo by Mary Elizabeth Kulesa, 2023. Courtesy of Clair Global.

WHY MUSIC?

Fig. 1: Frederick Powell, Street Music, 2nd & Chestnut Street, Philadelphia.
| ©Eric Zillmer, 2023

Fig. 2: Live Aid crowd and stage, July13, 1985.
| Image courtesy of Larry Magid.

GUITARS AND RHYTHM

Fig. 1: Jack Bruce's bass painted by The Fool, 1967.
| Image courtesy of Hard Rock International

Fig. 2: Jerry Garcia, ca. 1977–79, Spectrum, Philadelphia, PA
| Special Collections Research Center, Temple University Libraries, Philadelphia, PA.

Fig. 3: Croatian musician Ljubomir Vidović performing on a vintage double neck bass/guitar.
| ©Ana Vidović/Eric Zillmer, 1972

RHYTHM, POETRY AND LYRICS

Fig. 1: David Bowie performing at The Spectrum in the late 1970s.
| ©Eric Zillmer, 1978

Fig. 2: Carl Palmer, drummer for Emerson, Lake and Palmer, performing at the Spectrum in the late 1970s.
| ©Eric Zillmer, 1978

Fig. 3: Bob Dylan, Keith Richards and Ronnie Wood performing at Live Aid, July 13, 1985 JFK Stadium, Philadelphia, PA
| Special Collections and Research Center, Temple University

2ND ELECTRIC FACTORY

Fig. 1: Alicia Keys performing at Live8 in 2005.
|Photo courtesy of the City of Philadelphia, Special Collections Research Center, Temple University Libraries, Philadelphia, PA.

Fig. 2: The Starting Line fans Mike Golla, Kenny Vasoli and Matt Watts at the Electric Factory.
|Photo by Flickr user chriszak, © chriszak 2008, some rights reserved, https://www.flickr. com/photos/8154456@N03/2431843669/ Creative Commons — Attribution 2.0 Generic — CC BY 2.0

Fig. 3: Paramore performing at the Electric Factory.
|Photo by Flickr user kyle.tucker95, © kyle. tucker95 2009, some rights reserved, https://bit. ly/2NFnY4q Creative Commons — Attribution-NoDerivs 2.0 Generic — CC BY-ND 2.0

Fig. 4: Adam Spivak and Robert Plant backstage at Spectrum, Feb. 8, 1975.
|Photo © Roger Barone 1975

Fig. 5: The Live8 stage in front of the Philadelphia Museum of Art in 2005.
|Photo courtesy of the City of Philadelphia, Special Collections Research Center, Temple University Libraries, Philadelphia, PA.

Fig. 6: Will Smith performing at Live8 in 2005.
|Photo courtesy of the City of Philadelphia, Special Collections Research Center, Temple University Libraries, Philadelphia, PA.

LIVE AID, LIVE 8 AND FAMINE

Fig. 1: Drexel University students and World Vision staff members discuss water and sanitation projects outside the Hotel Amazin' near Bolgatanga, in northern Ghana.
|Photo by Idres Robinson, Office of Global Health, Dornsife School of Public Health

LARRY MAGID AND ELECTRIC FACTORY

Fig. 1: Mick Jagger and Larry Magid, Spectrum, Philadelphia 1981.
|Photo © Roger Barone 1981

Fig. 2: Exterior of original Electric Factory, c. 1968.
|Photo by Ed Carlin. Courtesy of the Atwater Kent Collection, Drexel University

Fig. 3: Allen Spivak and Larry Magid, mid-1970s, in the Electric Factory offices at 1231 Vine St.
|Photographer unknown.

ACKNOWLEDGEMENTS

THE IDEA FOR A SHOW ON ELECTRIC FACTORY

germinated prior to COVID, when Larry Magid offered to lend Drexel material from his own collection, reflecting his role at the heart of American popular music production over half a century. That initiative led to the present exhibition, made possible by his encouragement, knowledge and generosity.

The exhibition team extends particular thanks to Temple University, Larry Magid's alma mater, to which he gifted his original graphic material. Temple's Special Collections Research Center fully opened its doors to a sister institution. Bruce Springsteen, Hard Rock International, Rock & Roll Hall of Fame have lent important instruments to the show, and Clair Glabal and Paul Hammond made possible the concert stage component. Drexel's Music Industry Program and Fox Historic Costume Collection have also lent material, as have Drexel members Scott Hanson and Ed Zawora.

Electrified is an interdisciplinary project, mounted through the skills and knowledge of colleagues across Drexel University: in the Westphal College of Media Arts and Design (Arts Administration & Museum Leadership, Design & Merchandising, Digital Media, Graphic Design, Interior Design, Music Industry, Visual Studies); College of Engineering (Electric & Computer Engineering); College of Arts and Sciences (History, Psychological and Brain Sciences); Dornsife School of Public Health (Global Health); and Collections & Exhibitions in the Lenfest Center for Cultural Partnerships.

Jason Schupbach, Dean of Westphal College, and Sharon Walker, Dean of the College of Engineering, were enthusiastic and supportive.

The team offers special thanks to the University's Engineering faculty, staff and students who have graciously allowed this show to occupy their Bossone Research Center. The evolution both of electric musical instruments and high-quality concert sound is rooted in the innovations and problem-solving capacity of electrical engineers. Drexel students have also made valuable contributions, within Westphal College classes that used this exhibition as a teaching vehicle, and supporting the team during co-op, practicum, and work study assignments.

Drexel University is deeply grateful to the sponsors of Electrified: Ciright, Comcast-Spectacor, the Frank Barsalona Family, Philadelphia Music Alliance, Brian Communications, Red Spruce Capital, Saltz Mongeluzzi Bendesky, and Alan Kessler and Duane Morris.

Exhibition Team at Drexel:
Joe Amon
Chris Baeza
Kaisha Blackstone
Alissa Falcone
Valentina Feldman
Derek Gillman
R. Scott Hanson
Brandon Johnson
Youngmoo Kim
Dan Knittel
Nik Kozel
Mary Elizabeth Kulesa
Rebecca Lacher
Don Liberati
Sharukh Nayar
Leslie Quinn
Tim Raynor
Will Schumacher
Toby Seay
Aubree Snader
Emily Storz
Bill Swoope
Frances Temple-West
Fiona Tran
David Unruh
Lynn Waddell
Mark Willie
Pamela Yau
Ed Zawora
Eric Zillmer

PSYCHEDELIC SPONSOR
Ciright

SPECTRUM SPONSORS
The Frank Barsalona Family

Comcast Spectacor

Philadelphia Music Alliance

SECOND ELECTRIC FACTORY SPONSORS
Brian Communications

Red Spruce Capital

Saltz Mongeluzzi Bendesky P.C.

PHILLY MUSIC SPONSOR
Alan Kessler and Duane Morris

*Listing as of August 30